Teachers and Research

Language Learning in the Classroom

Gay Su Pinnell
The Ohio State University
Columbus, Ohio

Myna L. Matlin
Tucson Unified School District
Tucson, Arizona

Editors

International Reading Association
800 Barksdale Road, PO Box 8139
Newark, DE 19714-8139

INTERNATIONAL READING ASSOCIATION

Copyright 1989 by the
International Reading Association, Inc.

Library of Congress Cataloging in Publication Data

Teachers and research: Language learning in the classroom/ Gay Su Pinnell,
   Myna Matlin, editors.

   p.   cm.
Bibliography: p.
   1. Language arts (Elementary) 2. Language arts teachers – Training of. 3. Language arts (Elementary) –
Research.   I. Pinnell, Gay Su. II. Matlin, Myna. III. International Reading Association.
LB1576.T375   1989   89-15276
372.6 – dc19   CIP
ISBN 0-87207-350-5

Cover design by Boni Nash
Cover illustration by Lorraine Sebolt

Contents

Section Three Teacher Preparation and Professional Development to Enhance Language Education

Section Four Change through Extending the Knowledge Base

Appendix

Foreword

T he past decade has seen a consolidation of research evidence and of classroom experience to support the image of children as active constructors of their own knowledge. Whether it be in the early stages of oral language development, in the behaviors that characterize emergent literacy, or in the use of spoken and written language as a means for learning about the world, what is most apparent to those who observe young children at work and at play is their drive to make sense of their experience and to develop the competence necessary to achieve their purposes.

To recognize the autonomous nature of the child's search for meaning is not to deny the important role of other people in this process. However, what has changed over the past decade is our understanding of the way in which this role can best be played. Although in the past we tended to assume that what the learner needed was sequentially structured input and strongly controlled direction, we now recognize that knowledge cannot be handed over ready made but must be built up anew by individuals as they bring what they already know to the encounter with new information. In other words, the most helpful input is that which is contingently responsive to the learners' own efforts and which, in the context of a collaborative enterprise, enables learners to go further than they could have gone alone. The best teachers know likely routes to follow, but they lead from behind. In sum, we have come to see that the most effective model of the teaching-learning relationship is one not of transmission but of transaction.

To give widespread reality to this vision of education will require a major educational reform — one that will necessitate a change in beliefs, attitudes, and practices on the part of many teachers. The challenge is to find an effective way of bringing about this reform. In the past, attempts to bring about change in education typically have been carried out in a top-down manner. Experts outside the school have decided on the need for change and the form it should take and have handed their recommendations to the administrators. They, in turn, have drawn up guidelines for implementation and delivered them to the teachers who, after a few sessions of group inservice training, have been expected to put them into practice. Experience has shown, however, that this approach to change rarely is very successful. The reason, I think, is clear: A transmission concept of learning is no more effective in promoting learning in teachers than it is in the students they teach.

Perhaps the most important development of the past decade, therefore, is the recognition that the insights about learning and teaching gained from close observation of children apply equally to learners at any stage of development. If teachers are to create classroom communities in which students learn through active, collaborative inquiry, they must have similar learning opportunities themselves. This means a major rethinking of teacher education, both preservice preparation and inservice professional development. New structures will need to be found within which teachers can take a more active role in their own learning and in shaping the curriculum for which they are responsible. And those outside the classroom—teacher educators, educational consultants, and administrators—will need to rethink their roles in order to be able to support this process.

This, then, is the message of this book—a call for change at all levels in order to create the conditions under which learning can most effectively and constructively occur. But it is more than that. Not only do the various authors argue the case for change; in describing their experiences in classrooms, in school districts, and in university schools of education, they attest to its attainability and to the benefits for all concerned.

However, whilst there are those who will welcome the ideas presented here and be inspired to emulate the changes in practice that follow from them, there are others who will find them either threatening or offensive. As with every movement to loosen the grip of authority and to empower the disenfranchised, this call for a more agentive participation at all levels of education will arouse strong reactions from those who, because they subscribe to a transmission mode of education, have a vested interest in maintaining a hierarchical structure of organization and control.

Nevertheless, those of us who believe in these ideas can take courage from events in the larger political arena. In many countries around the world, there is an ever-increasing groundswell of popular agitation by people who are determined to take control of their own destinies and to attempt to acquire the knowledge and create the conditions to make this goal a possibility.

The parallel between national and educational politics is not inappropriate. Although quieter in tone and less likely to make the headlines, the chapters that make up this book are imbued with the same spirit and have a similar revolutionary aim. Let us hope that there will be many readers who, having gained a sense of what is possible, will be willing to join with the authors in extending and developing what they already have achieved.

Gordon Wells
Ontario Institute for Studies in Education
Toronto, Ontario

IRA DIRECTOR OF PUBLICATIONS   Jennifer A. Stevenson

IRA PUBLICATIONS COMMITTEE 1989-1990   John J. Pikulski, University of Delaware, *Chair* • Kent L. Brown Jr., *Highlights for Children* • Irene West Gaskins, Benchmark School, Media, Pennsylvania • M. Jean Greenlaw, University of North Texas • Margaret K. Jensen, Madison Metropolitan School District, Madison, Wisconsin • Edward J. Kameenui, University of Oregon • Charles K. Kinzer, Vanderbilt University • Christine H. Leland, Bridgewater State College • Ronald W. Mitchell, IRA • Donna Ogle, National College of Education • Timothy Shanahan, University of Illinois at Chicago Circle • Dixie Lee Spiegel, University of North Carolina • Jennifer A. Stevenson, IRA • Barbara Swaby, University of Colorado at Colorado Springs

Preface

T his volume, appearing ten years after the International Year of the Child, marks a decade of collaboration between the International Reading Association and the National Council of Teachers of English, a joint effort to bridge the gap between theory and practice. In 1979, the organizational alliance was forged, and a series of "impact" conferences were held in 1979 and 1980 to focus on the child in language learning.

Speakers at the conferences included researchers who had studied how children learn and use language and literacy. There were psychologists, linguists, psycholinguists, educators, and teachers. Professionals espousing different, even opposing, theories and having different perspectives on practice came together to discuss, argue, think, and learn. We had the opportunity to use language to learn together. Teacher educators talked about how to incorporate the new knowledge as part of preservice and inservice preparation programs and came up with ideas that were well ahead of their time when we consider the recent developments in teacher education reform. Teachers provided and demonstrated evidence of classroom experiences based on the new research.

These conferences were followed by a series of "strategies" conferences, which were held during the mid eighties. The strategies focus meant a more direct concentration on schools, on teaching, and on educational policy decision making. Researchers, teachers, and administrators formed a closer alliance and directed their attention toward influencing practice. Through the next several years, they worked side by side and attempted to reach out to others in the educational scene. In fact, much of the research reported at the conferences was conducted by teams of researchers and teachers. The concept of teachers as researchers and collaborators was born and grew strong during the years of the IRA/NCTE strategies conferences, and has now become the hottest topic in education. The results of the conference series continue to be visible in the groups of teachers, numbering in the hundreds, sometimes thousands, who regularly meet in large conferences and in small neighborhood gatherings to talk about children and their teaching. The work is evident in published newsletters, in publications from teacher researchers, in curriculum reform, in innovative teacher education programs, and in increasing concern for children at risk.

Teachers, researchers, teacher educators, administrators, and policy analysts are paying attention to language research, informing that research, and developing new perspectives on the effect of the environment on language learning. They are exploring ways to create supportive educational environments similar to the one the conference series created for its participants—with opportunities to use language to learn and, in the process, learn more about language.

This volume brings together for the first time in formal publication some of the landmark theoretical pieces that formed the foundation for the conferences. Works by Clay, Huck, and Goodman express ideas that forecast our work in educational practice for the future decade. In addition, the volume brings together new work from practitioners at all levels of education. The focus is on children. This book will provide valuable information for those engaged in creating educational settings that support children's development of language and literacy.

Dorothy S. Strickland
Columbia University

Bernice E. Cullinan
New York University

Yetta M. Goodman
University of Arizona

Sheila M. Fitzgerald
Michigan State University

Introduction

T he chapters in this book show that language and literacy learning are complex phenomena. As active agents of their own learning, children need thoughtful people to support their learning efforts; they need adults who encourage their attempts to make sense of the world. Children also need teachers who recognize how much they already know about oral and written language and who use that knowledge as a basis for creating educational settings.

The roles of teachers, researchers, and teacher educators/staff developers are interrelated; they all work within the same system. To achieve positive change, these groups must communicate and collaborate. We have designed this volume to exemplify the interlocking roles of researchers and practitioners.

This book contains four major sections. Each section begins with a brief commentary from a person who daily works with children, teachers, and school organizations. These "voices" from the field provide current examples of the impact of research. Other articles provide the conceptual framework, based on research and experience, upon which the theme of the section is focused. Articles also extend the theory to provide applications to research based practice.

The volume provides both personal accounts and theoretical perspectives for dealing with complex issues related to language research. Kitagawa, Platt, Milz, and Matlin and Wortman report personal experiences in classrooms as they grew in their understanding of how children become literate. Clay describes a specific approach to collaboration between teachers and university researchers.

After years of collaboration, teachers and teacher educators have renewed their appreciation for one another. They are willing to share their doubts about turning over control to students and their reluctance to accept changes required in their teaching strategies. Welsh describes her own change as a classroom teacher, while Jaggar reflects on the ways teachers learn and the implications for staff development. Huck outlines a graduate teacher education program based on an integrated model for learning.

It is clear that changes in literacy environments cannot be isolated in single classrooms. The effect of school policy and administrative guidelines has been demonstrated in numerous reports. Administrators and policymakers have joined in the collaboration efforts. In the fourth section, Monroe, as a superintendent, reports how school districts interpret, use, and create language research to make changes at the building and district levels. Pinnell develops a process for a school staff to examine and enrich the language/literacy climate of the school. Watson and Stevenson illustrate the change process by describing teacher support groups and networking systems. Finally, Goodman presents a concept of school practice as an expansion of children's language development. The voices of these teachers and administrators are convincing evidence of the necessity of developing new and strong language/literacy programs.

The book ends with a Suggested Reading List compiled by Jaggar and Harwood and with a list of references.

Preservice and inservice teachers will gain confidence from the reports in this volume. They will hear others speak with strong conviction, based on investigation by researchers and by teachers in their own arenas. Administrators and policymakers will understand the impact their work has upon the language/literacy programs in schools and communities. Researchers will see the difference between work imposed upon classrooms from the outside and that emerging from collaborative research. Teacher educators will gain insight about the future of schools.

Reading this book will require flexibility on the part of the reader. We move from intensely personal accounts embedded in daily practice to theoretical arguments to logical applications. That flexibility is required of all of us in creating research based practice. We are all colleagues; only by sharing our expertise can we make a positive impact on the educational setting we provide for children.

GSP
MLM

CONTRIBUTORS

Marie M. Clay
University of Auckland
Auckland, New Zealand

Kenneth S. Goodman
University of Arizona
Tucson, Arizona

Kathy T. Harwood
Woodhaven, New York

Charlotte S. Huck
Professor Emeritus
The Ohio State University
Columbus, Ohio

Angela M. Jaggar
New York University
New York, New York

Mary M. Kitagawa
Richey Elementary School
Tucson, Arizona

Myna L. Matlin
Tucson Unified School District
Tucson, Arizona

Vera E. Milz
Way Elementary School
Bloomfield Hills, Michigan

Donald S. Monroe
Winnetka Public Schools
Winnetka, Illinois

Gay Su Pinnell
The Ohio State University
Columbus, Ohio

Nancy G. Platt
Columbus School for Girls
Columbus, Ohio

Margaret T. Stevenson
Edmonton Public Schools
Edmonton, Alberta, Canada

Dorothy J. Watson
University of Missouri
Columbia, Missouri

Vida Louise Welsh
State College, Pennsylvania

Robert C. Wortman
Borton Primary Magnet School
Tucson, Arizona

Helping Children Use Language to Learn

Section One Prelude

C hildren learn language, learn through language, and learn about language. These three aspects of language development, originally conceptualized by Halliday in an address at a conference on "kid watching," represent key concepts for this entire volume. Detailed studies of how children learn language have extended educators' awareness of the complex processes involved in learning. This first section of the book focuses on helping children use language to learn.

We have recognized the importance of close observation. Kitagawa introduces this section with just such an observation and illustrates "learning through language" through the eyes of one child.

Language development is a complex process that cannot be observed directly or taught in a linear way. Language development requires opportunities to use language. Therefore, we need to construct educational settings that provide rich opportunities for children to use language in functional ways.

The educational focus is on content; language use and appropriate forms emerge from the study of that content, just as they do in the world at large. Platt helps us by describing what happens in such a classroom.

Observing Carlos: One Day of Language Use in School

T he sixth graders in my class began the day by working on self-
selected topics around a common theme. We live in Tucson,
Arizona, located in the desert, and my class of predominantly Native American and Hispanic youngsters was investigating various
water environments around the world.

Although they planned to write separate reports, both Carlos
and Alex chose to do research on the Florida Everglades, so they
sometimes compared notes. Carlos hoped to visit a relative in Florida some day, but neither boy had yet seen swampy land.

Finding Meaning through Discussion

On this particular day, Carlos asked me to help him understand a sentence he had just read in an encyclopedia. When he read
it to me, he stressed the word *and*: "Big Cypress Swamp *and* the
Everglades cover most of southern Florida." He asked, "Does that
mean that Cypress Swamp is not *part* of the Everglades?" I did not
know the answer, and I agreed with him that there might be two
ways to interpret the sentence.

Carlos called to Alex, and together they pulled down the wall
map of the United States. Although Big Cypress Swamp was not
identified on the map, the search seemed to give Carlos an idea. He
used the encyclopedia entry to trace a map of southern Florida
showing the extent of the Everglades. When I noticed how he alpha-

betically resequenced the entire set of encyclopedias as he put his volume back, I felt it might indicate how much he valued that resource because such meticulousness was not his typical behavior.

The two boys then leafed through an informational book on swamps, examining pictures and captions to decide which attributes might apply to the Everglades. I overheard them debating the extent to which the Everglades are covered by water. Alex speculated that they were all water, but Carlos said that his uncle had gone deer hunting there. "And, if he goes after deer, there must be dry land for the deer." When they found a picture of a deer in an area captioned as the Everglades, that settled the issue for Alex. Carlos wanted more evidence, however, and he returned to the encyclopedia. As evidence, he showed me a statistic describing the number of square miles of land in the Everglades National Park, but I explained that land in that sense meant area, including wet and dry parts. As I left the two boys, I heard Carlos telling Alex, "There's probably quicksand there, maybe."

Such informal conversations between the two boys and with me are natural in a classroom where talk and movement are related to learners' purposes. Had I been directing their inquiry, the interchanges would have been dominated by my leading questions and by my evaluative reactions to their responses. I might have sent the boys to look at the map or encyclopedia for an answer to a question I felt they should consider. But then the activity would have been influenced by its being communicated in "school talk" and by the fact that it was directed by the teacher.

In such exchanges, we generally limit talk about language to language class and rarely discuss it during science class. To deviate from this is to stray from the subject. Instead of being objects of inquiry, the ambiguities that Carlos discovered might have hindered his attempt to achieve factually correct answers to my questions. He probably would have guessed at an interpretation of the sentences in order to answer promptly; it is doubtful that he would bring the issue to his own conscious level, given the time constraints of such exchanges. If he did, my reaction as an authority would determine for him the accuracy of his guess, without our discussing it.

Finding Meaning through Text

By the time our paths crossed again, Carlos was using a third reference, another book about swamps. He showed me a sentence that led him back to the issue of Big Cypress Swamp: "Within the Everglades are two well known swamps, the Big Cypress Swamp and the Corkscrew Swamp." He and Alex went to the chalkboard and drew a circle to represent the entire Everglades, drawing within it two smaller circles marked BCS (Big Cypress Swamp) and CS (Corkscrew Swamp). Alex said, "Yeah, there must be tunnels that connect them."

Carlos sat down and quickly began to write his report.

> Florida's Swamps change alittle during the year. Swamps are grassey land witch water covers most of the time especially when it rains. The most well known swamps are the Big Cypress and the Corkscrew (sic).

In producing this lead, Carlos settled for himself the two issues that had occupied his attention—water coverage and Cypress Swamp. The rest of his report introduced the reader to the Seminole Indians, mangrove trees, and wildlife of the Everglades.

Finding Meaning through Vocabulary

After recess, Carlos, Alex, and the other students participated in a previewing discussion relating to a filmstrip about *Huckleberry Finn*. Carlos speculated that a "fugitive" might be a "prisoner." He knew, however, that "bounty hunters" would be "slave catchers" in this context. As frequently happens in school, we consciously studied vocabulary, taking teacher and student roles as in an English lesson.

As he watched the filmstrip, Carlos remarked upon the speed with which the story line was moving, saying that it must be leaving out a lot of the book. Carlos is a fluent reader who would appreciate the difference between a representation of a story line and the fullness of literary prose.

In the first scene in which a raft appeared, Alex brought up a text that various students knew, claiming: "The Kon-Tiki didn't have a rudder like that."

Carlos contradicted him. "Yeah, they did—a big log." Both boys had read a simplified version of *Kon-Tiki* and used the most exciting scene to create a play, which they performed for several classes.

Carlos demonstrated his ability to enjoy the literary diversity of language. I heard him repeat softly a phrase used by one of the characters in the filmstrip, "many and many a time," nodding as if that were safely immersed in his linguistic pool.

Rain forced an indoor recess, so Carlos kibitzed a chess game to equalize the odds of another child, a beginner, playing against the experienced Alex. Carlos was reluctant to explain aloud to his companion the rationale of his moves, however, complaining that it would tip Alex off too much.

Later that day we had storytime. When the phrase "one man's meat is another man's poison" came up in the story, Carlos jokingly speculated that it could be a warning against cannibalism!

Math was replaced by a special assembly with a former Peace Corps volunteer who had worked in Thailand. Carlos shouted out "Vietnamese" when the speaker asked what language is spoken in Thailand. Carlos looked embarrassed when he realized his mistake, but he recovered to name Bangkok as the capital. Previously, we had listed potential questions to ask the speaker; Carlos apparently kept tabs on these from memory because he commented as an aside during the narrated slide show, "He's covered just about everything we were going to ask him."

The last activity of the day was art. Carlos asked for pink construction paper in order to make a mask. Although I told him there was no pink paper in the supply room, he insisted on checking the accuracy of my statement. He found someone in the office to help him search, and when he triumphantly returned with a package of assorted colors that included pink, he said, "See, Teacher, you shouldn't give up so quick!"

Observation of Language Learning

These observations provide only a sampling of one child's language use for one day. I also was functioning as a teacher to twenty-seven other children and only informally keeping track of some tidbits of Carlos's interactions. I must have missed 80 percent or more of what he said, and I made little attempt to record what he heard, read, or wrote.

The structure of this classroom is internal; it is not often visible. Children are supported to direct their own activities in accord with their interest driven goals. The threads that provide social learning opportunities are the sharing of a broad, common theme, such as Water Environments, and the opportunities for peer interaction. In this format, Carlos and Alex were not interfering with one another when they communicated; they were mutually reinforcing the buildup of each one's conceptual and linguistic knowledge.

I directed their communication only a fraction of the time. Their self-direction led them more productively than I could have because they were actively engaged according to the range of their own interests. If I had overtly directed their research, I might have pushed Alex beyond his satisfaction with certain data or changed the subject before Carlos was ready to leave his line of inquiry.

Without direct instruction to do so, Carlos used language to represent information, to solve problems, to debate, to joke, to describe, to regulate others, and to make connections among various kinds of school and nonschool experiences. Throughout the day, Carlos focused on communicating and negotiating meaning with others, used language to solidify his own thinking, and focused upon language itself, as when he checked connotations or memorized a turn of a phrase. He used nonverbal symbolism to represent a concept to himself and to Alex; he used alphabetical order to organize a resource and often promoted his self-esteem by expression through language.

The written text he produced as a report was well done, but it represented only the tip of the learning iceberg. A major part of that data will be as fragile in his memory as the paper on which he wrote it, but he will not lose the ability to persist in the search for meaning. That is how language will serve him throughout school and beyond. If he has daily opportunities to practice both solitary and social interpretation of meaning through reading, speaking, listening, and writing in active engagement with ideas, he has the potential for lifelong learning.

What Teachers and Children Do in a Language Rich Classroom

O n a day in early spring, five first and second graders in Jeana Hodges's class in Upper Arlington, Ohio, were gathered on the floor around their large planning chart, trying to decide *what* to plant *where* in their class garden. With their teacher's help, they consulted a gardening book, looking at diagrams and sampling text. As decisions were made, children took turns labeling rows on the chart: spinach, $1/4''$ deep; radishes, $1/4''$ deep; and so on.

In collaboration with their teacher, these children were simultaneously learning language, learning through language, and learning about language. They were learning language by using it to listen, read, discuss, and decide on a plan. They also were learning through language about the world of gardening. Finally, they were learning about the nature and function of language itself. They realized that what they heard and said corresponded to what they wrote. They also were experiencing what language could do. In this way, they were confirming and extending their internal models of the functions of language (see Halliday, 1969).

Such events as garden planning served to carry these three aspects of language development forward, simultaneously and without direct teaching. Children were learning language naturally while focusing on meaning with little direct consciousness of learning or practicing forms. Instead, they concentrated on their projects and their friends.

The teacher had provided a social and intellectual context that supported language learning and use. She used resources of space, materials, and time to provide a homelike environment that was hospitable to children's needs to move, to rest, to interact, and to create. She planned regular literacy events which became so familiar to children that they could participate independently. Rugtime, the first event of the day, was followed by Worktime, a time of varied activities that often included writing. During Worktime, children wrote newsletter articles, trip permission letters, and self-evaluations. Observation Writing about plants and animals was a distinct literacy event, as was Reading Conference Time.

Each event had its own look and pattern of behavior. During Rugtime, children sat on the rug, loosely oriented toward the teacher as she shared information, led a discussion, read a story, or taught a song. In contrast, Worktime found children dispersed throughout the room, working alone or with others, moving as needed, deciding for themselves (within limits) what, where, when, and how to work.

During Reading Conference Time, all children were expected to read and be ready for a conference. Observation Writing saw children observing some bit of the world and writing their observations in their notebooks. Within this uniformity, however, there was flexibility. Children chose what to observe and write, where to work, and whether to work alone or next to someone. They were responsible for their own thoughts, wording, and transcription into written language. During Reading Conference Time, children were expected to read without disturbing others; however, they were free to choose their own books and places to read, alone or with a partner.

Because of the shaping of these familiar events, children had many chances to participate and to extend their oral and written language systems, both formal and functional. Thus, they were able to construct their own language system. At the same time, they were constructing their view of the world as evidenced by what they said and wrote during these events. Finally, by using language for different purposes in these events, they developed understandings about language itself—what it was like and what it was for. These understandings about language ranged from unconscious, implicit models of functions to self-conscious awareness of the surface characteristics of written language.

We will now discuss the way in which these literacy events furthered Halliday's three aspects of language development—learning language, learning through language, and learning about language.

Learning Language

Many of the qualities that support children's learning to talk in the home were characteristic of this teacher's classroom. Children conversed informally with one another and with their teacher, who responded primarily to their ideas. Children also were exposed to more complex and varied oral and written language to aid in their ability to understand others' meaning potential. During daily Rugtime, children heard sustained talk from their teacher and from invited guests such as a mother who was a scholar of Chinese and a father who knew about space travel. In this way, children were introduced to more formal oral registers and discourse structures and to many genres of written texts—informational books, biography, poetry, and extended fiction. These linguistic patterns and discourse structures appeared in the children's own writing:

> It is I, the great mayor of the town. I come because
> I want to visit your house.
> Warm yourself by the fire. It is cold outside.

While the teacher's more complex and varied language was beyond the children's present productive ability, she made this language accessible. She presented them with a clear sample, foregrounding important words and structures by intonational markers. For example, in introducing a selection about Benjamin Franklin and electricity, the teacher talked with the children, connecting what was new to what was familiar. She related ideas and language to children's concrete and social experiences; to classroom experiments with magnets, batteries, and bulbs; to kites; and to feelings about storms. By anticipating meaning before the children were asked to listen to the more formal informational text, she established a framework for understanding.

The teacher also made language accessible to the children by giving them many opportunities to hear new kinds of language. As they extended their language knowledge, the children began to discover the underlying patterns of organization. For example, near Halloween the teacher read aloud different stories about witches. They were not identical, but common terms such as *magic spells* and *cauldrons* emerged after exposure to a number of the stories, as evidenced by the witch stories the children wrote.

Children extended their vocabularies through this same inferential process. They learned meanings of words gradually over several encounters in slightly varying contexts. The meaning of *island* was not given by the teacher to be memorized, but it was inferred by children from a sequence of experiences—hearing the story about imaginary islands in *Elmer and the Dragon* (Gannett, 1950), seeing a filmstrip of *The Little Island* (G. MacDonald, illustrated by L. Weisgard, 1964) and reading the book afterwards, making a cooperative map of an island, and constructing imaginary islands.

In summary, the teacher helped the children understand more complex language by presenting them with clearly marked samples, relating the language to the children's familiar social and concrete experiences, and giving them multiple opportunities to discover the regularities of the language system. In these ways, the children developed a potential to decode others' meaning.

Children also were building their own meaning potential as they used language (sometimes approximate in form) to express their meanings and intentions through talking and writing. The teacher created situations in which children could use the expressive language familiar to them. In particular, she provided the key elements of purpose and audience. The children's own purposes, meanings, and intentions were the starting point. Those often were embedded in their active and social involvement in projects that the teacher had planned and the children had made their own—measuring the changing flagpole shadows in pairs, watching and describing "cloud pictures," or collaborating on an article about a favorite author for the weekly newsletter.

Whether oral or written, their language was responded to by an audience of their peers and the teacher. The others in their "meaning group" shared the given, often unstated part of their experience, and could understand their meaning. The teacher was able to take these sometimes implicit fragments and relate them to an overall, coherent theme, thus giving significance to individual children's contributions.

> The children and their teacher are talking about the inside of berries as seen under a lens.
>
> Child: We thought we saw...
>
> Child: ...a spider web
>
> Teacher: I know. It looks like there is something on the seed that looks like a little thread...it just looks like a little spider's web. We were wondering if the seeds were attached to something....

The teacher tracked the children's meaning and wove their metaphor into her own language, which she supplied to express their common observation. Like a parent, she joined them in the construction of language and meaning. This kind of response stands in contrast to the frequently heard pattern of question, answer, evaluation as documented by many researchers (Dillon & Searle, 1981; Edwards & Furlong, 1978; Mehan, 1979; Sinclair & Coulthard, 1975; and Stubbs, 1976).

The teacher's primary focus on intention and content meant that she accepted and supported children's approximations of form. For example, she often took dictation from children who could not supply their own form. Alan wrote "My Little Tree," and the teacher took down the rest of his thoughts: "My little tree's skinny branches wave their soft pine needles at the other trees. A little cat visits the little tree every day."

She also encouraged children to use their own resources to represent or placehold their ideas. Thus, Alan's next writing captured more of his meaning by the use of capital letters strung together, showing an emerging understanding of the relationship between oral and written language.

was transcribed by the teacher as, "I made a bloodsucker mask."

When children invented spellings, she commented positively: "I like the way you spelled *mashanarie* (machinery)."

One incident reveals her focus on children's intentions. When reading Sean's record of his rock weighing, she took his *wase* to be a misspelling of *was*, whereas he had intended *weighs*. She was dismayed about her misunderstanding, apologized, and then helped him relate the spelling patterns of *eight, weight, weigh,* and *weighs*.

The teacher accepted children's approximations, but she also helped them selectively to clarify their expression. She helped some children put more of their thoughts into words and others to move toward conventional punctuation and spelling. Her general method was to set up a clear paradigm from which children could draw out general principles.

> Teacher: (After talking about a child's ideas in the self-evaluation he has just written) I have a word I want you to spell for me. How do you spell *bone*?
>
> Steve: b - o - n - e ?
>
> Teacher: Now when you want to make a word plural, more than one, what do you have to add to it? What letter do you put at the end of a word when you want to make it plural? Like girl, girls; boy, boys.

These examples have illustrated growth of both formal and functional systems of language. Children needed new forms because they had to use language in a new way, for a new function. The examples show language in an informative function, one typically stressed in school. Children were not just interacting conversationally; they were telling or writing to others of their particular experience with the berries, the bones, the farm machinery, or the rock samples, In each case, language functioned to report to others through words alone.

This kind of language experience helped the children take a first step toward one goal of schooling: the ability to use language for increasingly abstract purposes and for unknown audiences. This first step was supported by the teacher's provisions for learning language, such as: a rich environment of oral language and written texts heard and read; familiar, interactive ways of working characterized by talk and action in concrete settings; purposes the children felt for using language; and audiences who shared their meaning, responded to their ideas, and helped them construct their expression as needed.

Learning through Language

While these children were developing their own system of language (or potential to mean), they also were building their own picture of the outside world by means of language. Children used language to talk about the many small experiences of their daily lives. In doing so, they were developing basic understandings about the nature of the world. Their attention was on their experiences — on birthday parties, math folders, lunch money, books, and butterflies — rather than on the language they were using to make sense of these experiences.

Everything their teacher had done to help them learn language at the same time helped them learn *through* language. She provided interesting, lively experiences with books, things, and ideas, which were available in varying forms throughout the two year period the children spent in this teacher's classroom. For example, concepts of birth and growth were gradually developed by theme studies of brine shrimp, gardens, and farm animals.

The teacher gave the children time and the opportunity to extend and internalize these new experiences through talking, writing, and playing, often joining them as a senior partner in their explorations. She also helped them to organize their experiences so they understood them better. For example, when planning their weekly newsletter, she helped them remember events of the past week and used their words to create on the board an outline of main ideas and subordinate points.

1. Lane Road Library Trip
   a. why
   b. when

c. what we need
2. Rocks and Fossils
   a. people sharing rocks, dinosaurs
   b. listening to tape
   c. word chart
   d. filmstrip
   e. looking at different rocks
   f. styrofoam Rex: 4½' tall, 6' long
3. Crystals—how we made them
   a. Gatheroo 12−4
   b. Toad—speedy
   c. garden—eating our peas

This outline served as a reference for children as they worked in pairs on their newsletter articles. It also demonstrated how to use language as a way of learning. In a similar way, the teacher helped children compile and order their observations and insights during the writing event. They contributed to group charts headed "Try My (Electrical) Experiment" or "Brine Shrimp Observations." They classified ideas with their teacher's help, making a chart of animal families—fathers, mothers, and babies—and a chart of the common features of different witch stories.

Finally, the teacher saw that children acted on these experiences and created their own products to represent learning. Their representations through painting, construction, drama, stories, and reports—no matter how fragmentary—were the teacher's window into what the children had learned of subject matter and of language.

An observation event illustrates learning through language. A small group of children and their teacher were gathered around a terrarium in which a toad and a chameleon were being fed mealworms. Children watched for about twenty-five minutes before they began to write one by one. During this time, there was opportunity to reexperience on a sensory level the contrasting appearance and behavior of these animals as they ate their prey—the toad lightning quick, the chameleon deliberate. Salient features of each were evident after many chances to watch these animals in action.

It is clear that both subject matter and language were being learned simultaneously. Children were forced to use their language to its utmost to express these perceptually complex situations. Through this process, they came to understand better the relationships they were striving to put into words.

For example, Ted's words helped him to appreciate a contrast he had arrived at after sustained observation of the two animals' ways of eating.

> The chameleon eats it with the side of his mouth and it hangs out....The toad just gets about this much away from it—and sticks his tongue out.

Ted's language helped him summarize his experience in a useful way. It is also possible that these concrete experiences, talked over and summarized, may have helped him develop such fundamental ideas as the relationship of bodily form to behavior and the survival of some animals by eating others. Both concepts seemed implicit in Ted's contrast.

How had the teacher interacted in this situation? A check of the first 4 minutes of the 25 minute episode shows that of 142 turns only 25 turns (18 percent) were the teacher's. During these turns, she focused on the group's shared interest in the terrarium, taking a collaborative rather than didactic stance. She explored and hypothesized along with the children. As the experienced member of the group, she showed them how to use language to notice phenomena, to question, and to discover relationships. As she observed, she remarked, "He missed it, didn't he!" or "Oh, there he goes!" She also directed children's attention to important features by questions and statements.

> Does he have little teeth?
> They look like little mealworms, don't they?
> Have you noticed how the frog and the chameleon differ in the way they eat?

After this extensive period of processing the experience by observing and talking about it, the children represented in writing what had been important for each. As approximations, they ranged from this faint echo of Cleo's vital talking and looking

> a menl Worm hAS
> 6 Laggs   Cleo, grade 1

to this relatively complete representation of Don's reality as he saw and struggled to convey it.

> The Chameleon Puts his
> head sideways before he
> attacks. then he Puts his
> head foward and open's his
> Mouth and gets him. then
> he leaves half out of
> his mouth the half he chews
> up and he swallows the chewed up part and
> sucks the rest and
> swallows it
>
>   Don, grade 2

The teacher could require all children to write these observations, thus ensuring regular writing practice for all; however, she could not foresee other spontaneous representations that appeared from time to time. Sometimes there was no outward sign of children's private experiences, such as when George gazed at a newly emerged butterfly or Tika sat for minutes absorbed in the progress of a mealworm moving across her palm. Often children shared their insights with no one in particular, as Ted did when commenting out loud that the little caterpillar in *The Very Hungry Caterpillar* (Carle, 1969) was like the seed in "The Little Red Hen," both being small and growing in importance. Mary wrote about the different size relationships of brine shrimp to their food and humans to their food.

> his Food is bigger then he is and
> are Food is not bigger than we Are?

She rewrote when adding to the class chart, manipulating language so that the second relationship was stated positively.

his food is bigger then he is and
we are bigger then are food is

Mary, grade 2

Ruth Ann's self-initiated retelling of "The Little Red Hen" was her own construction. It showed a variety of sources used to create a new world in the imagination.

> Turkey, Pig, and Little Red Hen and the Upside
> Down World
>
> One day a witch dropped a magic seed in a field but the witch did not notice. She rode on to Florida. One day Turkey was looking for worms. She found a seed. She called all the animals, "Horse, Hen, Pig, Goat, look what I found."
>
> "It might be magic," said Hen, and
>
> "Maybe we can become magic," said the Pig....

The teacher did not act directly to bring about this retelling, the spontaneous comparisons, and the time of reflection, nor could she have. She had made them possible, though. She had allowed enough time for unassigned as well as assigned activity. She had encouraged interaction and collaboration between children, and she had trusted them to decide how to use their time constructively. Thus, children had had time and opportunity to slow down and reflect on their experience by talking, reading, writing, and playing. Both verbal and nonverbal means were available to them. The teacher shared in these activities and through talk helped children discover order in their experience.

Gradually, within this informal, supportive setting, children were given experience with language itself as a powerful way of learning. They built a picture of their world by listening and reading, and they represented this picture in their own spoken and written words, gradually gaining in competence and skill.

Learning about Language

Children also learned about language, becoming gradually aware of it as an objective reality. While the network of social relationships and shared experiences engaged children's primary interest, they also could focus on the forms of language in an increasingly self-conscious way.

The teacher helped children learn about language through several familiar literacy events. She regularly worked with small groups on spelling or handwriting. She met with individual children in reading conferences. She heard children's compositions, responded to their meaning, and led certain children to discover selected principles of writing mechanics, thus increasing their awareness of the written language system.

Beyond these surface considerations, the teacher was interested in composing abilities such as audience awareness. When helping children select information for their newsletter articles, trip permission letters, or stories and reports, the teacher showed them how to think about what the audience needed to know. What did their parents already know about the chicks, and what new information should be included in this week's article?

The teacher furthered word consciousness by helping children learn new vocabulary and concepts in connection with each theme studied. For example, chrysalis, pupa, and larva were written on a butterfly shaped chart hung near the butterfly garden.

Beyond the word and sentence level, the teacher introduced children to new discourse structures such as biography and informational books (while continuing to read fiction and poetry). Children seemed to form implicit, internal models of these structures and were able to talk and write in the appropriate vein. For example, Evan wrote what he called "An Informational Book about the Booty (body)," and Mary wrote "An Informational Book about Animals."

Through their participation in such familiar literacy events, children learned about language itself. Evidence of this learning came from their informal talk and action, often while collaborating with one another. George and Sean discussed a newsletter article they were writing about their farm trip.

> George: How do you spell *soft*?
> Sean: S - A, O S - A - W K S - W
> Soft - AW AW...

On another occasion, Sean was working with Sam, writing about a tree they had just observed.

> Sam: How do you spell *had*? h - a - t?
>
> Sean: *Had*, not *hat*. That's *hat*.

Four girls gave one another spelling tests on the chalkboard, one dictating to another while two stood by. Cari told Caroline to write *squirrel*. Caroline tried: *swrl, sqrill, squr*. Cari said, "*Squirrel* is hard. You better look. You're going crazy with it."

Children proofread one another's work. Ken, Nini, and Daryl were jointly responsible for a newsletter article. Nini looked over Daryl's writing and said, "That doesn't make any sense," referring to an unintended grammatical garble caused by repetition. Ken came over, helped Daryl, and dictated the next sentence.

Children tried out wording, as Ted did when formulating his mealworm observation: "Should I say 'before he catches'?" Mary and Cynthia were writing about an author, similarly searching for words to use. Cynthia said, "How about 'he illustrates books'?"

The children also served as audiences for what the others had composed.

> Monique: Ok, Mary, Mary, let me read this to you.
>
> Mary: I'm listening.
>
> Monique: "We went to Ruth Ann's garden this week, this week. And everything is growing. Something was nibbling on the pea plants."
>
> Mary: Good. Listen to mine. "As you know, we are having a Gatheroo on May 31 from noon to four. There will be twenty games, there will be twenty games and jewelry too. You know, we had it last year."

Children also thought about higher levels of language organization, as Mary and Tika did when planning their roller movie. They were dealing with story structure when they decided upon the scenes in "The Lamb and the Colt."

While children made books, they talked about the process of assembling them with the pages in order, and the need for a cover and a title. Books were a concrete and familiar embodiment of written language.

Reports and informational books were written and referred to as such. While looking at a photo of a friend, Deborah revealed her concept of a report.

> There is Hannah writing a report, I think. Like Mrs. Hodges puts a sheet of paper and we write down things that we can do on it and then we pick a project that we want to do and we just write it, do it.

Finally, many unofficial projects showed the children becoming at home with language per se. In this classroom, the children often wrote on their own initiative, making scrapbooks, reports, lists, and surveys, as well as writing notes to their teacher and friends. Two girls made tiny books of "secret writing," which fit inside little pockets inside folders in notebooks. The girls were playing with concrete and linguistic material, making or creating something satisfying in itself. In the process, they were focusing on language and books for their own sake.

In these ways, the children seemed to be increasingly aware of their language, especially in its formal aspects. Yet although they talked about spellings, even wordings, they seemed unconscious of the functions of their language. This unconscious knowledge of function was probably the most powerful knowledge of all.

Over their preschool years, the children had built relevant internal models of what language was for and could do (Halliday, 1969). In this classroom, these models were still relevant. The children could wonder and ask why; they could play and create with language; they could use language to share their own feelings and establish connections with others; and by means of language alone, they could let others in on their ideas and learn of others' lives (Halliday, 1975).

Thus, the children's early experience of what language was for could be confirmed by their school experiences. Early functions, particularly the use of informational language, could be continued and extended. The children were put in the position of independently conveying experiences through language itself. Often matters were more abstract and audiences more distant. This solo structuring of text, more difficult than cooperative conversation, was balanced by the continued provision of familiar situational elements — of concrete tokens that stood for ideas and of familiar, first audiences of teacher and peers who understood the writer's background and gave the writer's meaning a place in the meaning of the whole.

Children continued to develop knowledge of language use at an implicit level. This unrecognized learning about function was nonetheless critical, as it led to learning language and learning through language. Children who talked and wrote for a variety of purposes were also building, revising, and refining their language system and their internal view of the world. In addition, they were gradually becoming aware of the system they had built and what they could do with it.

Section Two

Teacher Development through Involvement in Language Research

Section Two Prelude

T he key to positive change in language/literacy education is increasing the professional knowledge and practical skills of teachers. We see children as active learners who increase their understanding through investigation and construction of meaning. This process is assisted and affected by interaction with others. In other words, they use language to learn. Typically, teacher learning is seen as listening to lectures, perhaps with some discussion, or reading materials. If we wish to seek a model for teacher development that is consistent with our view of learning, we need to find activities that allow investigation and collaborative learning.

In this section, we examine the researcher role as one that has great potential for teacher development. First are some comments from Milz, a teacher who takes a researcher's role in her own classroom. Next, Clay presents a conceptual framework for involving teachers in classroom research with examples from her early intervention program, Reading Recovery. Finally, Matlin and Wortman illustrate how teachers and researchers can work together, with each enhancing the work of the other.

3

Vera E. Milz

Comments from a Teacher Researcher

A s a classroom teacher who is also a researcher, I have found that productivity and effectiveness in one area are enhanced by activity in the other. Through my own research, I have become aware of what is happening in my classroom and have gained confidence in the children I teach and in my own power to teach. As a teacher, I confirm what I read in research journals, put the research into perspective, understand it better, and criticize it when necessary.

I am curious about everything children do. In that sense, I always have been a researcher. I knew interesting things were happening in my classroom and was dissatisfied with the status quo. Before I started formal research, I traveled to England and observed writing among five and six year olds. I thought, "If they can write so naturally, so can the children I teach." Children are not all the same; they don't fall into slots. Yet, we keep trying to force them into programs where they all do the same thing without looking at the ways that children learn language. I began by trying new things, recording the results, and observing.

Research in the Classroom

My main focus as a researcher has been on the development of children's writing. I wanted to find out what was happening to young children in the beginning stages of becoming writers. For years, children had written for me, and I had saved stories and messages. I found that I could look at the writing of children over time and begin to find the reasons for and the logic behind what they were doing.

For example, in one study I looked specifically at six children who had similar birthdays. After examination, I realized that these children were very different from one another. One child used patterned language; another used invented spellings. Different children were reaching out to communicate. At times they looked similar, and I learned that I could see growth patterns, but these, too, were highly individual. Even children who were at roughly the same stage could not be treated exactly alike. I learned that I could not give the same writing assignment to twenty children and give them a limited time to complete it. All children communicate through writing, but each one needs to have ownership and purpose in the task.

What does teaching contribute to my role as a researcher? I can look at children in greater depth than can most researchers. I am with the subjects six hours a day, for an entire school year. I am responsible for their learning, an aspect that gives me different insights from those of an outside researcher. As a teacher, I also have control over the environment, and because I can structure learning experiences as needed, I can take more risks in the interests of research and have confidence that what I am researching is being implemented in the classroom. Researchers often have one treatment in mind, but classroom teachers can implement something subtly different from what researchers intended.

Being a teacher helps me as a consumer of research. I read articles and take them to my classroom to look for confirmation in the behavior of the children I teach. I can compare the progress of individuals with the "stages" identified through statistical research and thus gain perspective on my reading. Observation of my own children helps me to better understand research. For example, I remember reading Read's (1975a) work on young children's spelling. Many children had spelled my name "Mes Mez," and I wondered why they spelled it that way. When I read the research showing how children make their own sound analysis, I knew that was what my students were doing. Connecting scholarly work to my own work with children helps me to understand the research and increases my awareness of what is happening in the classroom.

How does being a researcher help me as a teacher? I constantly describe and analyze the environment in which I am living. I confirm and rework my own beliefs about children as they grow and develop. I gather compelling evidence of children's learning and talk about it to administrators. My principal has always been very supportive, and the evidence that I gather is a very important reason for that support, especially in circumstances where I want to depart from established or traditional practice.

Research Yields Practical Benefits

As a researcher, I can look at instructional materials and analyze whether they meet the needs of the children I teach. I can eliminate ineffective materials or use them in more effective ways. I have this independence because I can explain what I am doing, and I can uncover evidence as to whether something is working or not.

Research gives me more confidence in the children and in my own teaching. I can recognize progress and make decisions as to the children's needs. I do not have to teach to a test that is going to be given in January. I know they will perform well on tests because they are learning.

This evidence of learning is important in talking with parents. At meetings with parents, I present information gathered over the years that will help them look at their own children's development. I show transparencies of writing samples that offer specific examples of the kind of learning I am describing. I show how children invent spellings as they begin to write and then gradually become more sophisticated as they move toward standard spelling. I explain how I work with the children and offer evidence of their progress. Parents can see and understand the progress. I show materials their children are reading and provide examples to show how they are reading it. I point out behavior that indicates children are looking for meaning and solving problems. I tell the parents that they may see some of these behaviors in their own children, and because I have evidence of learning, parents are supportive. The more they see and understand what is going on, the more they help.

Knowledge is a powerful tool for teachers. My own knowledge of children's daily reading and writing gives me greater confidence and satisfaction in what I do. I am always searching for new ways to learn. As a teacher, my own experience suggests that the teacher's researcher role is a productive and rewarding one that has possibilities for enhancing both research and teaching.

4

Marie M. Clay

Involving Teachers
in Classroom Research

A t first glance, the title of this chapter seems redundant. How could one do classroom research without having teachers involved since teachers would inevitably be doing the teaching? In the research community, the topic may not seem to be promising. What self-respecting researcher would want to deal with the unpredictable events of a real classroom? How could any sound research design hope to discipline the multitude of factors that enter into the daily interchanges of teachers and pupils? In this chapter, I will discuss the benefits to researchers of involving themselves in classroom research.

Are teachers already doing research? Almost everybody claims to "do research," from the television program assistant to the mothers' play group committee to the political campaign committee. Research has come to mean the gathering of relevant information. If we limit the term to mean projects that employ the scientific method, then I would suggest that the essence of the scientific method has been observation rather than experiment. We then can ask whether teachers are engaged in observation in their day to day teaching activities. The answer must be affirmative, because each move a teacher makes while teaching is the result of observing the responses of the students to a previous move.

So experienced teachers are already sensitive observers. Their attention is not on this observation as such but on the trajectory of the lesson. With experience, teachers perceive, pick up, intuitively appraise, and subjectively monitor the responses, products, and progressions made by their pupils without giving too much thought to the process of observing. In these respects, teachers are different from the scientific observer who sets up a particular situation in order to record, with precision and objectivity, exactly what occurs.

I do not think we can say that teachers in their day to day activities are already doing research in the sense of making objective recording of practical settings. It is a short step, however, for teachers to move from being intuitive observers of teaching and learning to being objective and reliable observers in the scientific sense. They must step aside from their teaching roles temporarily, and they must receive some training that includes sound observation procedures.

Teachers already are good at taking into account the many variables that affect the teaching/learning situation. I do not claim that teachers are articulate about all variables affecting classroom research, but in working with teachers, I have found that they are often the ones who raise the critical issues. They understand the implications of differences in abilities; they understand pupil variability, realizing that today's efforts may not be as good as some previous work; they have an excellent grasp of the progression that pupils must make as they climb ladders of difficulty in various subject areas; they understand the school year calendar and its implications for the timing of the observation; they are aware of the times when extra pressures or demands fall on teachers or pupils; and they understand some of the variables that arise from the teacher's level of experience, as well as that good teaching comes in different forms because of teacher differences.

I believe that teachers are masters of the complexity of their tasks; they have a good, if intuitive, grasp of the changes that occur in pupils over time, and they understand a great deal about the interaction between teachers and pupils, which is, after all, the essence of teaching. Researchers, on the other hand, have difficulties with all of those areas – complexity, change over time, and interactions. It seems logical to examine how difficult or easy it is to bring the two professional perspectives to bear on the single problem of classroom research.

There are some difficulties; one is the bias that arises from personal experience. It is inevitable that what we believe about children comes from some pooled and averaged summary of our experiences with children. Teachers' experiences have been limited to children in certain locations, at particular class levels, or of certain ability levels. As a result, teachers judge a new program, research finding, or discussion of educational objectives in terms of their experience. This introduces some bias in their judgment.

Researchers have limited personal experience, but they reduce bias by using rigorous procedures, such as choosing children who represent a wider sample or choosing samples with known and described characteristics. In the latter case, the researcher knows that the findings apply only to other groups of children of like characteristics and that they must take care in reporting findings.

A second type of bias comes from our belief systems. Teachers cannot teach without believing in the value of what they are doing. They are constantly confronted with choices. Will we use this material or that? Which of two activities will best achieve our objectives for the children? Which curriculum change has the greatest potential for my class or school? Such questions are decided in part by the educational values we hold and the educational goals we aim for.

Researchers also have belief systems derived from the competing theories in psychology and education, and those beliefs are formulated as theories to be subjected to rigorous tests. A result cannot be attributed to the program being tested until it is shown that it could not have occurred by chance. In the case of an equivocable result, the researcher cannot believe one possibility and forget the other. A test must be devised to address the question of which of the two possibilities is bringing about the effect. To move forward in a discipline, the researcher must question beliefs, but to effectively teach, teachers must adopt beliefs. Thus, teachers involved in research often must take on new roles that are not typical of the involved and inspired teacher.

One other difficulty is associated with the outcome of research. Teachers usually think in terms of a new procedure, a new program, or a new concept of goals. They would like research to help them handle the complexities of their work, the changes in children over time, or the minute by minute interactions of teaching. For the teacher, a research outcome may be good because it works, and the teacher may have a number of plausible explanations as to why it works. The researcher's goals must be quite different. The researcher must achieve a general formula that will have applications that are far wider than the particular classrooms of the teachers he or she has worked with. The researcher's task is to question theory and provide new statements of theory that can be refined by further questioning. Researchers deserve some sympathy because they have to talk to both the teachers and to their colleagues, whose roles are not to praise and admire but to search for weaknesses in the research. Knowledge is assessed by such public appraisal.

Teachers and Curriculum Construction

Teachers' perspectives are valuable in conducting classroom research, and it makes sense to involve teachers in the processes of evolving new curricula. Whatever the role of specialists in subjects and in curriculum design, teachers who represent those who will use the new scheme in their classrooms can make an important contribution. There is a tradition in my country for consulting teachers and having them serve on committees that work on curriculum revision. Teachers also are involved in piloting the new programs and reporting on them. Such processes seem to have two main advantages. First, they insure that the new ideas will be workable in practical settings, and second, they make communication with teachers about the new ideas easier because the curriculum designers already have faced communicating with teachers on their committee.

Consultation with teachers who know the complexities of the practical scene can be most helpful to the curriculum designer. Communicating to educators and teachers will be easier if their perspective has been understood.

Teachers as Data Gatherers

I am interested in how children's behaviors change over time—the sequences they pass through and what encourages shifts to new levels of achievement. To study change, a researcher must have some way of gathering data at regular intervals. I encourage teachers to develop ways of capturing change in their pupils, mostly by collecting and saving samples of work and comparing several pieces for differences.

At one time I was interested in samples of children's writing. Because I already had some hypotheses about the progressions made based on a small group of children, it was important that I use a large, random sample and collect early writing in all its varied forms from child to child and school to school.

I purchased some unlined exercise books, wrote some simple directions, and asked teachers to have their students write their daily stories in my book on one day in the middle of each week. They were to do this every week for forty weeks. As a result (allowing for absentees, mobile families, and interruptions for unusual events), I gathered nearly two hundred books filled with interesting writing by children in classrooms. I had done almost nothing; the teachers had gathered the data. However, they had gathered it under standard conditions, which meant that I could pool the material and analyze it for common sequences of change.

A second example of using teachers as data gatherers occurred in twelve surveys of what children are like at the end of elementary school in New Zealand. We asked them to write about their out of school activities, interests, and perceptions of their world. On a particular Monday morning, teachers in one-third of New Zealand's elementary schools gave their twelve and thirteen year old students one of our twelve questionnaires. Six weeks later, the teachers administered the questionnaire a second time to check on the reliability of the data.

School principals had the right to refuse to participate, as did teachers. Yet, the cooperation was superb throughout the entire country, and we believe that most of the teachers followed our instructions about administration and anonymity, sealing the envelopes in front of the pupils immediately after the forms were completed. Teachers in hundreds of classes issued thousands of forms consisting of millions of questions. They were cooperative data gatherers.

In both examples, two factors were important in gaining cooperation. First, the purpose of the research was explained to the teachers, and they saw the researcher's goals as similar to their own. They had an interest in finding out about changes in writing over time and about the out of school activities of their pupils. They considered the research relevant to their own professional needs.

Second, the task was a simple one designed to fit easily into the busy life of a schoolteacher. It involved minimal time and effort on the part of the teacher. As a researcher, I always have considered myself to be an intruder in the teacher's realm—an intruder whose presence costs the teacher time, disruption of the program, and anxiety. I like to maximize my use of the data collected by teachers by designing my research well, asking the teachers to do only what is feasible and reasonable, and feeding back to them any information I gain as soon as it is available. If they let me intrude into their territory and time, I owe them an early return of information in a usable form.

The Teacher and Systematic Observations

I'd like to mention three different approaches to systematic observation. In contrast with casual observation, the systematic observer has some procedures and categories to guide the observations. One of my research students recorded exactly what happened during a whole morning in ten infant classrooms, using a strict time schedule to redirect her attention every ten seconds to the teacher or to pupils. She used a complex set of categories for recording the activities, the size of the group, and the responses of the children (Watson, 1980). Systematic observation schedules are not for the lazy.

Another approach to systematic classroom observation has taken its methodology from anthropological research and has resulted in the writing of a running account of what is occurring, trying to characterize the social climate, the demands and expectations, and the responses of teachers and pupils.

Yet another approach has asked teachers, by way of a questionnaire, what their beliefs about teaching and learning are and has followed with observations in the classroom to see how the teacher uses that philosophy in practical activities.

Researchers who use a behavior analysis model sometimes work in classrooms and involve teachers in their research. In global terms, and without going into detail, they are typically invited into a classroom by a teacher who defines a control problem with particular children or an academic problem in a particular subject area. The analysts would make some systematic observations using a reliable method, which would give them a natural history report of how the class responds to the teacher's efforts. They call it a baseline study.

The researchers may then discuss the graphs of these observations with the teacher and discuss some ways in which the situation may be changed. When all agree on a strategy, the teacher can be encouraged to continue as before, altering one aspect of teaching behavior, the program, the teacher's control, or rewarding behaviors. The researchers continue to make observations and capture any change that takes place.

This process continues with small changes and renewed observations until a satisfactory degree of change has occurred and class responses have become more satisfactory to the teacher. The changes that achieve any degree of stability are those that are acceptable to the teacher and that result in better responses from pupils. Teachers who have participated in such research become interested and eager colleagues of the researchers, willing to carry larger research loads than might be expected. The approach involves a great deal more than training teachers to increase positive and reduce negative reinforcement.

Teachers and Research Planning

I mentioned earlier a series of surveys that New Zealand teachers gave to children who were around twelve years old (Clay & Oates, 1984). One fine teacher helped me with that research project. Together we reviewed the literature, examined the available surveys, designed new ones, and planned the sampling. In addition to organizing the distribution of 40,000 questionnaires to schools, he helped in planning the research. In our discussions, he would often politely, but firmly, signal disagreement. To my academic researcher's biases he brought a thorough knowledge of both the urban and rural schools of my country, of the viewpoints of teachers, and of what is feasible within the schools' timetables.

He was often able to predict that some of our questions would draw facetious responses from the age group and was able to suggest alternative formats. He told me when I was introducing a feminine bias or stereotype of boys, and I would reciprocate if I thought the masculine tone of a question was making it inappropriate for girls. The same processes were operating when we came to the interpretation of the data and the writing of the report. Those surveys would have been less appropriate and would have had less chance of engaging the cooperation of the teachers and the children had I not had the benefit of a sensitive teacher to contribute to the planning and management of the project.

Some Personal Experiences

In classroom research there are two major types of questions we can ask. One type relates to the general query "What is teaching?" and the other type relates to "What is learning?" or "What does it mean to be learning a particular subject?"

Some people ask what theories we have about teaching or about learning, and their research flows from that question and is designed to answer that question. Some people ask what programs teachers are using and how they are implemented, or they may ask how well children are learning in two different programs. Those questions determine the choices of research strategy available. Then there are two questions that are more open and not closely related to any particular theory: "What do good teachers do when they teach?" and "What do children do as they learn?"

The emphasis of my early research in reading was on "What do children do as they learn to read?" I felt that we had not written the natural history of learning to read. There were many theories and much tightly controlled research, but what actually happened as children moved into reading and progressed into more difficult reading? I took a sample of 100 children and recorded what they were doing as they read, every week for the entire first year of school.

At first I had a small area of concern. If I watched the children's progress closely, would teachers fear that I might uncover their weaknesses? This concern was overcome by sharing as many of my findings as feasible as soon as possible, rather than waiting until the final report was written. In that way, both the teacher and I were focusing on the child, sharing our professional knowledge for the child's benefit. I also talked to groups of teachers about the progress of the study.

I also had a second area of concern. A natural history of what happened should coincide with what sensitive and observant teachers already knew, so I ran the risk of being told that I was contributing nothing. My argument for the teachers was that I would not be discovering anything that a good teacher who had experience with first year infant classes did not already know, but I hoped that what I wrote would have two uses. It should put into some articulate form what teachers already know intuitively, and it should make this information available to inexperienced teachers and even to teachers in training. Teachers seemed to accept this description.

First, I decided to study the outcomes of the teachers' efforts in terms of what the children were doing. Then I talked with teachers and shared my information as far as I understood it in an ongoing project. When I came to my conclusions, I tried to find out how teachers would interpret what I was saying. Then I conducted workshops for those who wanted to study the outcomes of their own teaching.

How could teachers become observers? I had worked out ways that I had found easy and useful for recording what children say and do as they read, and I offered these researcher's tools to teachers. The tools were not sophisticated psychological instruments requiring specialized training; they were standardized situations. The recording required some skill, but it could be learned.

Teaching can be improved by systematic observation—patient, painstaking efforts to record what exists without bias or distortion. Images of the botanical drawings of Victorian times created as a scientific record come to mind. With these convictions, it was natural to invite teachers to adopt the scientific method, to become careful observers, and even to use some of their busy and precious teaching time for nonteaching observations. I felt that kind of research would lead teachers into new understandings of children.

How the Reading Recovery Program Evolved

When we looked at the children having difficulty (and the teachers insisted that we help them with this problem), we based most of the study on observations of what good teachers do when they work individually with a child who finds a task hard.

I began with one good, young, and not very experienced teacher whose master's degree thesis had dealt with reading. She was very sensitive to the children's problems. She had practical teaching experience, but she also was able to articulate in terms of theory what she thought was happening in the learning-teaching situation. This teacher was the first of many to be put into a very difficult situation. From one side of a one way screen she taught a child who was virtually a nonreader. From the other side, I watched and recorded the child's responses and her teacher initiated moves. Sometimes the child's parent or class teacher would watch with me.

When the teacher had finished, we would have a long discussion in which I would go over the lesson and ask what she thought happened at a particular point, what she thought the child's problem was, and why, in theoretical terms, she had taken the action she did. Hers was not an easy task, and many times she would say, "I knew you were going to ask me that, and I'm not sure why." With the press of the teaching situation, we make quick decisions, and it is confusing and frustrating to be asked for a reason for the action.

We struggled through these sessions and seemed to reach some clarity about two things: the children's difficulties and the teacher's responses. However, she was only one teacher, and I was only one observer. Often we did not agree on the articulation of what was happening, but our personal biases were being built into the program. We needed more teachers and a wider range of children.

About this time, two Department of Education reading advisers asked for our conclusions about handling children with reading difficulties. I answered: "We do not have a clear idea of where the project is leading us, but by the end of another year we might be ready to begin writing our report. If you'd like to join the project, by the end of the year you will be as well informed as we will."

They joined the project along with two reading teachers and one teacher of infants who had become a full time university student for a year. Now we had six teachers, five who taught two children each throughout most of the year and one who taught six to eight children. Each teacher had to agree to teach on one side of the one way screen for the benefit of the other teachers, who observed and discussed what was happening from two points of view—the child's behavior and the teacher's behavior.

By the end of the second year, we had a range of responses from children with different kinds of reading difficulties, and we had several approaches to solving those difficulties that we had gathered from the team of teachers. The first teacher on the project and I tried to put these ideas into a simple guidebook for use in the third year.

We could proceed two ways from this point. Continuing to use teachers with specialized experience in a laboratory setting, we could show that the procedures raise children to the level of their classmates. Or, we could show that teachers without specialized knowledge could make this scheme work in ordinary school settings. I had enough confidence in what I had been observing and in the teachers in the field to believe that the second approach was the one to use. If we could demonstrate that satisfactory gains could be made in the schools by teachers, perhaps our results would be acceptable to educators.

We wanted an everyday, practical scheme for schools that would not be unduly demanding of resources, and we wanted to show that the scheme did not require my supervision or vast resources. With the strong support of the District Senior Inspector of Schools, we already had found the funds to pay for the first teachers on a part-time basis for two years. We applied for, and received, five teachers to use as we chose.

We selected some schools from low socioeconomic areas with average to below average attainments, and we talked with the principal and some staff members. We explained the project and said that we would like the principal to release from class teaching a good, experienced infant teacher. One of our allocated teachers would be given to the school to take the released teacher's class. The Reading Recovery teachers would teach children individually throughout the year. These teachers had four to eight years of experience and no special training in reading.

This was the framework with which they had to work. In New Zealand, children begin school on their fifth birthday, so that when each child had been at school for a year, the Reading Recovery teacher checked the child's reading with a set of observation procedures. From those results, the children who most needed attention were selected for the Reading Recovery teacher's program. We made some rules. The children should be given a full lesson of about thirty minutes each day, and the teacher was not to be taken off the task for any other school activity.

We left to the teachers certain things which we expected to vary from school to school. They were the researchers in this case. By the way they dealt with these problems, they showed us some of the possibilities and limitations of operating the scheme in schools of different sizes with different ethnic groups and different types of home backup. The teachers decided on the following factors.

- Which children would come into the program?
- Would they have two short lessons, one long one, or some other arrangement?
- How many weeks would the children stay in the program?
- When would children be ready to discontinue the supplementary program and be able to survive back in their classroom?
- What particular reading materials would suit each child and what particular activities would be introduced into the required slots in our program?

On one thing they had no option. They were to teach and reinforce the children for using strategies – operations carried out in the head to solve problems regarding print. They would expect comment from their peers at the observation sessions if they seemed to be teaching for items of knowledge such as letters, sounds, or words rather than for strategies.

To our surprise, the teachers demonstrated that daily individual lessons could lead to nonreaders rejoining their class activities with competent performance at an average or better level after about fifteen weeks. Some took longer, and some took less time, but these early successes meant that the teacher could now take on more children.

In all these activities, the teachers were teaching us many things. They came to an inservice session once every two weeks. Two of them demonstrated a lesson with children they had brought in, while the others watched through the one way screen. Their tutor and I would deliberately begin to discuss the child's difficulty or the teacher's particular choice of teaching task. Before long, our teachers were also discussing in the same way, and I could hear them articulating the kinds of things my first teacher and I had sorted out two years before. Their leader led them to new questions and new insights. In the hour that followed the lessons, they discussed their own children's puzzling behaviors and difficulties they were having in understanding some of the procedures or rationales we were working on.

One main focus was the guidebook that my first teacher and I had carefully written at what we thought was an easy level. From time to time, the teachers politely made it clear that the guidebook was not guiding in some parts and was plainly confusing in others. They were invited to tell their tutor every time they encountered a difficult, unclear, or inconsistent sentence or passage, and the tutor wrote every complaint against the offending passage in the guidebook. At the end of the year, the guidebook was covered with comments, and a complete rewrite clearly was needed. We asked the teachers for their suggestions for making it more understandable, and they were able to suggest the inclusion of examples in some parts and changes of order in others.

Let me recapitulate what had happened in the year of field trials. We let the principal choose the teacher; we let the teacher choose the children; we let the teachers arrange their timetables and their ways of working; and the teachers chose the activities and materials through which they would achieve transformation of the children's skills. We also let the teachers use the teaching procedures and skills that they were successful with at first and only gradually introduced new ways of teaching with rationales that arose in discussion, allowing the teachers to take on new concepts and procedures at their own rate. If they were too deviant in their practices, the comments of their peers pointed this out in group discussions after the demonstration sessions.

If our goal had been only to discover what range of organizational and teaching materials were used, how the ability levels of the children admitted to the program differed between small and large schools, and for how long the average program would run, then we had to let the teachers determine these factors in the research program. Those, however, were secondary research questions. The major research question was, "Could teachers working in this way recover children and return them to their classrooms to work at average levels?"

We were depending on these teachers without research sophistication to support all our hypotheses about the early intervention program. We might have used highly trained university graduates to effect the changes. Instead, we worked with the teachers and provided support services to introduce techniques, foster discussion, and monitor decision making. We allowed the teachers' peers to support and to challenge them whenever they were able. Consequently, we achieved a double payoff from the program — children who could cope with their classwork and teachers who were excited about what they were doing.

In the following year, we ran an inservice course for fifty new Reading Recovery teachers, divided into four groups. Again we found that teachers worked very hard to understand the new teaching procedures. They kept the few rules we set. They made the program work in schools that were very different. They became enthusiastic about their work, and educators who saw them at work commented on their delightful teaching. Visitors to the inservice sessions (including important administrators) sat on high stools behind the teachers who were observing the demonstration. They were enthusiastic observers of the two levels of tutoring they could see at one time—a teacher tutoring a child on one side of the one way screen and a teacher trainer tutoring the teachers on the other side of the screen.

You might think that at the beginning of the school year we should give our teachers an intensive training program so they would do only the "right" things. We chose a different strategy. Teachers were reminded that they were experienced educators and were urged to draw on their own experience when working with children. We did not wish to undermine the confidence of these teachers by lecturing them on a new approach.

We considered it economical to gradually move children and teachers from present competencies rather than to demand immediate new behaviors that would cause confusion and disrupt established and efficient responses. Teachers began the first lessons using their own prior skills before any new teaching procedures were introduced. Gradually, new concepts and activities were demonstrated, discussed, and made part of their teaching. As the course continued, it became obvious from the teachers' discussions that their concepts of children's tasks and of their own roles had changed.

From the beginning our teachers had their own theories about the task and pupil characteristics. By the end of the year and after the inservice course, they had acquired new theories about these two areas of performance. They questioned, challenged, discussed, and worked out a course of action, and they explained their decisions in ways all could understand, because the theories were shared and explicit. They did not always agree with one another's decisions, but they could communicate about them.

At the end of the school year, we asked the teachers to write their reactions to various aspects of the year's work. You will recall that teachers brought in a pupil and taught before peers. None enjoyed the demonstration situation, but almost all commented on its value, using words such as: valuable, great, useful, excellent, helpful, exhausting but valuable, absolutely necessary, and stimulating.

Teachers described their experience and what they had gained in these ways.

- I found it a nerveracking experience demonstrating and not much easier the second time.
- I dreaded bringing a child in and being observed, but it was a valuable experience. It got easier as I went on.
- The one way window was invaluable and could never be replaced by videotapes. Being able to see someone working and being able to discuss and question as they went along was really good.
- I learned so much by just observing the children at work. Each one is so different, and how they operate on print can vary so much.
- I was reinforced in some things I was doing and at the same time was shown ways of improving and new ideas.
- The sessions taught us a lot, made us more aware of what we were doing and more self-critical.

The emphasis in the latter part of the year shifted to the most worrisome pupils who were having the greatest difficulty. In their demonstrations, teachers were asked to teach in ways deliberately chosen to expose the child's peculiar problems to the group. Afterwards, in discussion, the resources of all the teachers were directed toward exploring the problem and searching for solutions. The teachers' comments reflected the value they found in this part of the course.

- The most difficult pupils are very interesting to watch.
- The last term, when we saw people working with very difficult children, was extremely helpful.
- One of the early demonstrations should be with a child who knows almost nothing. Where do you start? What do you do? How do you build on nothing?

Demonstrations were followed by an hour of discussion. Topics included the demonstration just completed, teachers' own cases, difficulty with a particular concept, questions about variations of procedures, and appeals for suggested activities or materials for particularly unresponsive child. The comments on these discussion showed that teachers had a need to discuss their own work; i.e., "There was never enough time to talk about everything that happened."

Reading Recovery teachers needed to meet other Reading Recovery teachers to air problems and find possible solutions. As a result of these discussions, they recognized changes in themselves.

- I can honestly say that I learned something new every time I went.
- A major percentage of learning takes place here. The in-service sessions extend and consolidate understanding of reading processes and recovery procedures.
- They kept me thinking about ways to improve my teaching and gave me a good opportunity to discover whether I was approaching problems in the best way.

What we now need to recall is that this research was not deliberately designed to effect changes in teachers. All I have been describing was what was happening to our research assistants and others who carried out the program in the schools. The research question was "Could we take the end of the normal distribution of reading ability after one year of instruction and put most of the children back into the mainstream of class teaching?" We, as researchers, did not do that. The teachers did it, and they did it with such success that our analysis of the results showed that the effects were not only greater than chance but also greater than regression to the mean, a statistical problem that remedial programs often cannot beat.

Summary
I have been closely involved with the project featured in this chapter. I know that in the United States there are research projects that involve teachers in the classroom. When researchers become excited about kid watching, they cannot help introducing teachers to the same exciting opportunities. A review of the impact of research

on policy and practice in education gives two very strong arguments for such cooperative efforts (Nisbet & Broadfoot, 1980). The first argument points to the retarding effects of old ideas on new developments.

> Research shapes values (and practices), but when it moves ahead, it is constrained by the context which it has created.

You may recall how we moved our reading advisers along our discovery path by asking them to join the project. The second argument for cooperative effort is this.

> There are different stakeholders for different areas of research...but if research is to have impact, it must become participatory, involving stakeholders in the research process. When clients or practitioners have different values from researchers, these values will operate consciously or subconsciously to deter them from commitment, and thus limit or prevent impact.

Myna L. Matlin
Robert C. Wortman

5

Observing Readers and Writers: A Teacher and a Researcher Learn Together

T his chapter is our reflection on what was gained through our collaboration as a researcher and a teacher during a one year observational study of young children learning to read and write. The research was designed to study literacy development of young children in school. We gained a greater understanding of literacy development, and of how we as educators and collaborators learn and make changes. The first section is written by the researcher, the second by the teacher.

From the Researcher's Perspective

Locating the right setting for the research was important, so I interviewed several teachers and talked to many university and district colleagues. Two basic issues needed to be resolved before I could invite a teacher to participate in the research. One issue was my strong interest in focusing on students' literacy development rather than on a particular method of teaching reading. I wanted to observe what children do naturally when they are asked to read in a supportive, homelike, literate environment rather than to see how children respond when teachers ask them to sound out words and letters or to read in some other specific way. The other issue involved the definition of the population: Who were the young school aged children to be studied? Were they to be five year old emergent readers, as many educators refer to them (Holdaway, 1979) or older six year old beginning readers, as they have been defined in school (Smith, 1965, 1986)?

These two issues were resolved when a colleague phoned to say that an outstanding whole language teacher was to have a combination kindergarten and first grade class for the following school year. Almost immediately, the collaboration began. The teacher and the school principal were responsive to the suggestion that a research study be conducted in his classroom, although the teacher was apprehensive of being observed so closely. I emphasized that the observation would focus on students, and that observation of teacher strategies would be noted only in relationship to interactions with students as they read and wrote.

For me as a researcher, this setting and collaboration proved ideal. My intention of studying literacy development was supported in this setting because of the nature of whole language classrooms. Here, children interact with both oral and written language in natural, unsegmented contexts much as they do outside of school. The emphasis is on students' learning rather than on teachers' methodology.

> Whole, meaningful texts are the instructional materials, not
> isolated words, sounds, or vocabulary controlled "stories."
> In a "whole language" classroom, oral and written language
> must be functional, fulfilling a particular purpose for the
> language user (Edelsky, Draper, & Smith, 1983, p. 259).

In a whole language classroom, I could focus on literacy learning in the most "natural" setting that could be provided in public schools in the United States.

In addition to providing a naturalistic setting, the collaboration influenced my research in many ways. The teacher's knowledge of his students and his support for the research added an insider's view that enhanced the study through

- the sharing of background knowledge about students,
- the providing of a rationale for his interactions,
- the recall of anecdotes from times when the researcher was not present, and

- the explanations of how materials were used and why these particular ones were selected.

Background Knowledge about Students. Since the teacher had been in his present school for several years, he knew his students, their older siblings, and often their families as well. His relaxed, friendly relationships with the families provided access when permission was needed for the children to participate in the study and again when it was time to collect interview data regarding literacy events at home. He knew how and when students had interacted with print at home during their preschool years and, now that they were in school, how they interacted before and after school and on weekends.

One example of this knowledge emerged when I was attempting to figure out how an experienced five year old reader was not able to read the label for a Campbell's product. The teacher knew the family well enough to know that all their soups were homemade, and this fact enabled me to infer that the child had limited past experience with this item.

The teacher also knew his students well because he was with them for five days each week, five and a half hours each day. In addition, he had taught the first graders as kindergartners. He knew how they approached literacy tasks, how they worked with adults and other children, and how willing they were to take risks. Obviously, this extensive knowledge was greater than I could gather in the two or three mornings a week I participated in the setting. This shared information about the literacy learning of the five and six year old subjects was a strong support for the data collection.

The teacher also demonstrated a remarkable ability (which all good teachers must have) to know exactly what was going on in the classroom at all times. While I would come into the setting each time to look closely at the print interaction of one child from the study, the teacher seemed to know what other students were doing as well. At the end of the observation, a few moments of discussion were shared, and I always came away with additional data. For example, I would be told to look at Steven's journal, or that Fernando was following the print while the story was being read on the tape recorder.

Most important, the teacher knew about five and six year olds. He knew what to expect, when they needed assistance, and how to give it so that their learning was within their zone of proximal development (Vygotsky, 1977). That knowledge had many consequences for my researcher's view of teaching and learning, but the most important was that it allowed me to study the children in a naturalistic setting. I was able to see how they continued to learn about literacy in the same ways as before they came to school. They expanded their experience and knowledge; the teacher was the facilitator of that expansion. The focus was always on the children.

Rationale for Classroom Interactions. It was possible to gain an inside view of the classroom because the teacher was articulate about his goals and planned interactions with students. When he made on the spot decisions, such as whether to take dictation from a student, he talked about his reasons, and I was able to see why the action was taken. In addition to my own data, this accessibility of the teacher's view of the child's learning gave a fuller picture of the young children's developing literacy. As a teacher and as a researcher we had different and equally contributing perspectives: one as facilitator and evaluator and one as observer.

Anecdotes. As the research proceeded, the teacher became an integral part of the project. Before long, he and I met regularly to discuss classroom interactions and to share anecdotes indicating children's learning. Teachers record anecdotes on students' permanent records for future teachers to study, and they also share anecdotes and samples of students' work with parents to show growth. Researchers, using ethnographic techniques, take anecdotes from research protocols to elucidate data and to bring reports and papers alive. So the sharing of anecdotes in this project was a natural situation. It was especially helpful to me to hear from the teacher about the many literacy events that occurred while I was not present in the classroom.

Selection of Materials. The selection of instructional materials is an important aspect of the job of any teacher—particularly a whole language teacher. The availability of a wide range of functional reading and writing materials seems to stimulate students' purposeful print interactions. The teacher played an equally important role in working with students as they interacted with materials. His explanations concerning why certain materials were selected and how they were used proved to be valuable information. In addition, he was able to inform me how the subjects from the study dealt with various printed materials in the classroom. He noted which materials were causing difficulties for certain students and which were being used successfully.

Without the knowledge of the classroom teacher, the data collected would have been less rich, less powerful. The young literacy learners presented in case studies in the research were better understood because the collaboration created a sharing of information that described each subject better than any one person could.

From the Teacher's Perspective

From my perspective as a teacher, having a researcher in the classroom affected many aspects of my program and of the daily life in my school. Curriculum, classroom environment, evaluation, and people outside the classroom were influenced by the collaboration.

Curriculum. Because someone was in my classroom to study reading and writing, the focus on literacy was intensified without a deliberate plan to do so. Shifts in levels of attention happen in most, if not all, research settings, but are rarely acknowledged. It became important for us to state this fact and to use the strength of the collaboration to extend our own knowledge in order to participate more fully in children's literacy development.

As a teacher who had already integrated language learning throughout the curriculum, I became more aware of how extensively my students interacted with print. It was reassuring to discuss classroom interactions with another educator and to read written summaries that verified the extent of my students' participation in literacy events. I also used information from the protocols to provide for new opportunities for learning when I discussed strategies with students. Literature books became a central focus around which the curriculum was based, and extended teaching units were developed.

As information was shared and I observed the researcher interacting with students, I decided that I needed to spend more time interacting with individuals. If I, as a teacher, could provide the same type of sensitive interaction as parents give to children at home, children's learning about reading and writing at school would be enhanced. In addition, writing became a stronger component in the literacy program because I could see evidence of relationships between the reading and writing processes emerge from the researcher's field notes.

As in many classrooms, reading had played a major role in the written language program. Now I attempted to balance reading and writing so that students would have an opportunity to "play" with print, that is, to learn more about writing as a process of meaning making and to learn more about the orthographic system of their language. As these five and six year olds observed the teacher and researcher asking questions about their writing, they began to read one another's writing, and child generated discussions of process and product ensued.

The focus on literacy had an impact on students. Once they became aware that some students were spending time reading and writing with the researcher, it was not uncommon for her to walk into the class and have students not participating in the study show her their latest draft of a story or ask to read to her. The tape recorder, introduced early in the school year for listening and recording, became a more common part of the program. Children would read stories into the recorder and ask others to listen. During the school year, most students requested a private interview with the researcher. Reading and writing were affirmed as important classroom activities and integral parts of the learning environment.

Classroom Environment. An important part of the collaboration came in the form of sharing journal articles. I asked for research articles to improve aspects of the classroom literacy environment, and when the researcher read an article she believed would be of interest, she passed it on to me. When either of us attended professional meetings, research presentations were discussed. From this sharing of information, I undertook a study of the literacy environment in the classroom. While I always had many types of books and reading materials available, I began to organize the classroom with more functional uses of print in mind. Charts, labels, recipes, and comics, along with books, notebooks, magazines, and newspapers, were given recognition as instructional materials. Enjoyment, recordkeeping, communication, and learning were seen as meaningful functions of written language.

The supportive affective environment of the home became my model for print interactions at school. My role as teacher moved toward the role parents fill at home—nurturing and accepting children's written language. Learning opportunities became more individualized and cooperative, as has been observed in homes where literacy interactions are part of the natural learning context (Doake, 1981; Taylor, 1983).

In discussions, we noted the time and attention children spent on their own literacy development. Young children have notorious reputations for short attention spans, yet my young students were working for an hour or more on projects that needed completing. By observing students, I decided to expand the morning work time to allow for more interaction and to give students time for self-correction and extended learning.

Evaluation. Research protocols based on the ongoing case studies, written language samples, and miscue analysis provided the basis for many of our discussions (Haussler, 1982). I began to realize that my input into the discussions was needed because of my strong background in "kid watching," a term coined by Yetta Goodman to describe the classroom observation of students for qualitative analysis of their learning. It became apparent that my observations were more global than the researcher's. I had a sense of what was going on in the whole room, while the researcher could thoroughly describe what one child had done during a morning. I decided I needed to focus on giving more individual attention to each child's learning.

Although it was not easy for me, I began to carry a clipboard to make notes to myself during the day and to keep samples of children's work. There were at least three ways this form of record keeping helped. First, I had a record of children's strengths; I knew which children needed to continue working independently and which needed individual or group attention. Second, it encouraged me when I felt that a child was not making progress. I could look at the notes or samples and see that progress might be slow, but it was being made. Third, I had concrete examples to show parents when we had conferences. Parents' reactions to seeing their children's development were always positive, and I assured them that their children were developing school literacy.

One particular event helped us to realize that the social context of the classroom was mirrored through the observation of individual students. I was talking to two six year olds about their writing. After the content was discussed, I held an impromptu language lesson. I wrote out the words *to, two,* and *too* and talked to the boys about what each means and how it is spelled. Both had confused these homophones in their writing. The researcher took notes on the interaction, and afterwards I commented how pleased I was to have been with the boys at this particular "teachable moment," when they were ready to learn these concepts.

Over the next two weeks, the researcher noted that at least four other children attempted to experiment with the forms of *to, two,* and *too.* Notes of the original event showed that only two of the children could have been close enough to have heard the interaction. We assumed the children had been helping one another, and this was confirmed over the next few weeks as information, not always correct, went around the class to other students.

People outside the Classroom. The most surprising aspect of our collaboration is the influence it has had on others outside my classroom, including teachers, the principal, and parents. Teachers asked questions about what it was like to have someone writing down everything that was going on in the classroom and listened when they were told "it really wasn't that bad." They also began to take an interest in lunch time conversations and to share anecdotes and innovations from their own classrooms. The school librarian photocopied bibliographies and research articles for teachers to use and ordered new materials for the professional school library. *Language Arts* and *Young Children* were put on a table in the teachers' lounge to be read and discussed.

Noting the growing interest in literacy development, my principal requested that the researcher provide an inservice session for the staff. The principal also used documentation from the research findings to support my nontraditional classroom environment and discussed these findings with other district administrators.

All of the parents were interested in feedback about their children and particularly enjoyed seeing examples of their progenies' reading and writing. Most voiced interest in the concept of research in the classroom; they believed their children would benefit from the experience and were as anxious to talk with the researcher as they were to talk with me. Two parents were motivated to learn more and took a class about written language development offered at the local university.

Summary

Not all collaborators will benefit from this type of experience as much as we did, but it was a positive learning experience for both of us. We brought unique perspectives and knowledge to the classroom research and, as a result, we learned from one another.

For the teacher, observational skills have become more focused. He now believes that his teaching style has changed and grown and that he has improved in his ability to articulate a rationale for his holistic approach to literacy education. He has grown professionally, as he has presented at local, state, and national meetings; talked with other educators in his district; and worked with students and their parents.

For the researcher, it has been an opportunity to learn more about teaching from a model who seemingly knows "how to do and observe three million things at once." She has learned much about how and why five and six year olds read and write in a natural social context where first hand observation and description were possible. Her observational skills were improved throughout the course of the study, and her qualitative analyses improved through discussions with the classroom teacher. Both have become friends and colleagues who have learned from one another. Both will be able to use the information learned during this study to improve learning for others — especially for young readers and writers.

Section Three

Teacher Preparation and Professional Development to Enhance Language Education

Section Three Prelude

I mproving language/literacy education means changing language/ literacy education, even in the case of programs that already are pretty good. This means change at all levels of language education, from preschools to the preparation of teachers. The articles in this section illustrate that change is difficult; it takes time and hard work. Individuals must grapple with their own previous beliefs and understandings; they must cope with new ideas that are threatening to the established and comfortable attitudes; they must build new belief structures. Welsh's vignette is an honest account of change from the perspective of one teacher. Jaggar presents a conceptual framework illustrated with her own problems in achieving a coherent theory. Huck describes an educational experience that will help prospective or inservice teachers to develop new understandings.

A Teacher's Experience with Change

I once was asked to talk about my experience as a classroom teacher who had gone through a major change in my teaching situation. After accepting the invitation, I wondered why I didn't feel more excited. It was flattering to think I might have something worth sharing with other teachers, but I thought the wrong person had been selected. I wasn't supportive of the changes taking place in my school. In fact, I was outspoken in my criticism of them. Wouldn't it be better to have one of my colleagues who had been quick to see the potential of this new program speak instead of me, the reluctant dragon?

As I wrestled with this idea, I realized I probably had been invited because of my initial reluctance. Why did I offer so much resistance to something I now regard highly? I have given this much thought and concluded that there might be a lesson in my struggle, a lesson for teachers and for others trying to make changes in our schools.

Initial Resistance

One July day several years ago, I found myself seated across the desk from the head of my school. Seated next to me was a reading specialist who had conceived a new reading program. There was an air of tension in the room as they expressed their fear that I—because of my position as grade level chairperson and senior faculty member—would sabotage their plans.

Their thinking resulted from events at the end of the previous school year, a year which ended with an emotionally charged meeting of the faculty. Along with several other faculty members, I had spoken out against the change being implemented. The meeting ended with the decision, made by the school head, that the following September a pilot group at each grade level would use the new approach to reading. The results would be carefully monitored and, in the spring, a decision would be made about broader implementation. It was not clear exactly who would make the decision.

"Why should I change what I have been doing successfully for many years?" I had courage enough to ask that question. More burning questions were: "Why are you doing this? What are your motives? Does this change really represent progress in education, or is it being done for political, empire building reasons? How is this program, which requires a great expenditure of time, energy, and money, going to do the job better?"

To understand my dilemma, you must understand that I love teaching and I love the school where I teach. I have taught there for many years and have seen many changes. I have worked under five different heads, taught three different grade levels, and been housed in two different buildings. Important to the situation I am describing is the fact that I feel a tremendous sense of responsibility for the children I teach. I believe that teachers can have a lasting influence on the lives of their students, and I consider it my moral obligation to provide them with the best program and the best materials I can.

There is evidence to substantiate the fact that I am a successful teacher. I am respected by my students, their parents, and my peers. I have worked hard to perfect my teaching. At this crossroads in my career, when I was being asked to change, I was proud of my accomplishments. I had been through many changes, but none had caused such a spirit of rebellion in me.

In *The Creation and Setting of Future Societies*, Sarason points out a fallacy in society's concept of schools—that schools exist *only* for children. Schools also are settings in which professional adults hone and buff their craft. After many years of honing and buffing, I was being asked to change.

No longer would I use a published program, prepared by the experts. From this point on, my colleagues and I would create our own programs, design our own activities, and be totally responsible for the focus, scope, and sequence of the reading program. If this was a "better" way, it must mean that what I had done in the past was negated—that I hadn't really given my students the best possible program. This personal conflict engulfed me. I think other teachers who are asked to make significant changes struggle in similar ways, and this inner struggle is an important factor for change agents to consider.

The following is a chronology of events and pertinent factors that established the reading program now used at my school. These events initiated the internal conflict I've described. Some of these events inflamed the conflict; others helped resolve it.

The woman selected by the board of trustees to head the school was a forceful, dynamic leader who stated that her goal was to create the best private day school on the East Coast.

After spending a year becoming familiar with the school, she hired a specialist to coordinate the reading program on all three campuses. The reading specialist spent a year looking at the program being used and meeting with department heads and faculty. She presented research from the National Assessment of Educational Progress which indicated that children in the primary grades scored well on achievement tests, but these achievement scores made a dramatic downward turn in the middle grades.

The information had little impact on me. The grades I taught were doing well, and I didn't see the connection between what I was doing and this research, which seemed to indicate difficulties in the middle grades. There was a connection, but at the time the information was not presented in a way that helped me understand the need for change. In addition, resources in my school were limited. Whether to use the resources for administrative salaries or to supplement classroom materials and teacher salaries was an issue among the faculty as these reading specialists were hired.

The professor responsible for creating this new approach to teaching reading addressed the faculty, presenting the philosophy behind the program. The specific details of the program and how it would be used in the classroom were saved for a workshop to be held at the close of school.

I looked forward to the workshop. I had a thousand questions about this program that had not been answered by the philosophical presentation. Conducting the workshop was an educational consultant who had never taught, and while he was familiar with the program, he was not especially knowledgeable about the teaching of reading. As the workshop progressed, an air of tension and hostility developed between the "expert" and the faculty. The need to change had not been clearly established in my mind, and this workshop did nothing to convince me that the program under consideration was better than (or even as good as) the one being used.

Establishing pilot groups became another emotional issue. As mandated by the head of the school, there would be a pilot group at my grade level. Only one teacher volunteered to teach the pilot group, a teacher who had just been assigned to fourth grade. Previously she had taught kindergarten. I did not trust the motives of the change agents, the need to change was unclear, my first exposure to the program was negative, and the initial implementation was to be done by a teacher new to the grade level. These factors explain the air of tension that existed at the final faculty meeting.

Teachers who had volunteered to implement the program the next fall worked intensively with the reading specialists for five days after the close of school. They ordered materials, organized the curriculum, and discussed plans for classroom management. (They were paid for this additional work.)

In September, the pilot groups went into operation. Special memos were sent to parents informing them of the program. The teachers were well prepared, and the program was impressive. A great effort was made to communicate to the rest of the faculty what was happening in those classrooms. Visitation of these pilot classes was encouraged by providing free time so teachers could have first-hand exposure to the program.

A Change of Heart

This period of time marked a turning point in my own thinking. Before my eyes, I could see some wonderful things happening.

At my level, the teacher was enthusiastic, and the students were happy and productive. Best of all, students were becoming more involved in their own education. My reservations about this approach to reading began to melt, and I wanted to learn more about it. The pilot year was successful in convincing faculty, students, and parents that the new approach to reading was educationally sound and more desirable than the program previously used.

At the end of the year, the reading specialist wrote a formal proposal. Another workshop was organized, this time with an experienced teacher of reading who was also familiar with the new approach. Through some creative scheduling, demonstration lessons were taught at each grade level with all faculty at that level present to observe. Immediately following the demonstrations, teachers discussed the lesson and asked questions.

This demonstration workshop and the success of the pilot groups converted me. I realized that supplementing the basal program with literature (my own approach) did not have the potential of this new approach that used literature as its core. Trade books replaced basal readers, and workbooks were replaced by group and individual projects related to the books.

Throughout that spring and summer, there was tremendous support from the leadership team and the administration. The school provided funds for teachers to purchase needed materials and to attend workshops and take college level courses. A spirit of commitment and sharing developed within the group. No question was too trivial; no doubt ignored. Everyone pulled together to solve problems like organizing time, keeping records, reporting to parents, covering skills, evaluating materials, selecting classroom libraries, and adjusting this program to the special needs of our student body.

Our reading program has come a long way since that beginning. It is fully operational at the primary school and making progress through the middle school grades. A colleague of mine at the upper school spent a year on full sabbatical to work out plans for changing the focus on reading and writing at that level. He spent a considerable amount of time in my classroom and others at the primary school learning our program and how it could be adapted to the upper school. Later, a workshop was held for faculty, consultants, and students from the upper school.

This is no longer the creator's program; it is unique to our school. The program has been supplemented with a special component in writing. It makes use of the computer as a tool in teaching language arts, and it has been integrated with social studies and other content areas. It has changed the atmosphere in the classroom from one where quiet, passive children seek information from the teacher to one where active learners make decisions, ask questions of themselves and others, and take responsibility for their own learning. Additionally, the new program redefined the teacher's role from director of activities, checker of workbooks, and keeper of order to that of a facilitator and observer who provides strategies and confers with children to help them discover what they know and how they are going to proceed.

We are proud of our program. Faculty support for the system continues. There are weekly grade level meetings with the campus reading specialist and monthly reports from the leadership team. Faculty development continues, because the administration recognizes such activity as a critical ingredient of success.

Summary

What can we learn from the story of this one innovation? This must look like a well orchestrated plan, and it was. Initially, three factors caused a breakdown in the plan. The first was trust. The school administration had not established rapport with those being asked to change. Although the head of the school was energetic and innovative, she had not convinced me of her dedication to high educational standards. She was in a hurry to improve the school and made top down decisions without involving the faculty and allowing ideas to evolve from the bottom up.

In *Teachers, Their World and Their Work*, Lieberman (1984) writes

> Teachers are at the core of any improvement effort. We must pay attention to their personal and professional concerns, and the ways in which they function as a separate culture in the school.

Leadership is essential to innovation, but education does not happen in the superintendent's office; it happens in the classroom between teachers and students.

The second factor, which in a way relates to trust, was the need to change. Conscientious teachers invest a tremendous amount of themselves in what they do. Mandating them to change dramatically, without firmly establishing a rationale, is not likely to breed success. Finally, once teachers see a need to change, they must be presented with an alternative, a better way.

If I had sat quietly, not resisting or questioning the innovation or the change agents, I probably would not be as enthusiastic about this program as I am. By airing my doubts, resisting the current of events, I called attention to these flaws—trust, the need to change, and a better alternative plan—in the implementation, flaws which otherwise might have gone unaddressed. That July meeting gave me the opportunity to verbalize my reservations and my professional conflict. I would not have sabotaged their efforts, but I would not have put my time and energy into making the program a success. I came to the understanding that acknowledging the merits of this new program did not negate what I did in the past. I was true to my craft then because I gave my students the best I had. Now, I have grown and see a better way of teaching, and this improvement is confirmed by my students' actions and comments. For example, as the bell rang at the end of the school day, Robyn looked up from the book she was reading and said, "Mrs. Welsh, is it time to go home already? I just got started with this book and I don't want to stop yet!"

When you get to the bottom line, teachers make or break a program. If they believe in what they are asked to do, if they are given opportunities to verbalize and resolve their professional conflicts, if they are supported rather than dictated to by the school leadership, and if they are sufficiently trained, the program will succeed. If those ifs are not met, interest in the program will stop outside the classroom door.

7

Angela M. Jaggar

Teacher as Learner: Implications for Staff Development

W hen I was asked to write about the Teacher as Learner, I was reluctant because I thought a classroom teacher rather than a university professor should be the one to talk about how teachers learn. I mentioned my dilemma to Yetta Goodman, who looked at me and said, "You are a teacher. Why don't you talk about how you learn?"

I am a teacher. I have taught most of my life, first as an elementary school teacher and for nearly twenty years as a professor. Although I do research and a myriad of other things expected of university professors, I get my greatest satisfaction from working with teachers at the university and in the field.

I agreed to write about the Teacher as Learner for two reasons. First, I had been doing a lot of thinking about how I had changed over the years—how so many of the things I talk about and advocate in my language arts courses are different from what I did when I taught third and fourth grade in a school in Long Island, New York.

Second, I had been speaking and writing about how to improve instruction based on all the exciting things we had learned in the past decade about the nature of language and how children acquire and learn to use it. Yet, numerous reports, along with my own observations, confirm that, for the most part, the materials and practices in use in our schools today are at odds with the best that we know about how children learn to talk, write, and read.

In education, practice has always lagged behind theory and research. It takes time to get new information to teachers, program planners, and others responsible for classroom practice. But as McCutcheon (1982) wrote, "no longer does just a *gap* exist between theory and practice; we currently seem to have a Grand Canyon" (p. 46). Why does the gap exist? As Huck (1982) has warned, other forces are at work. Mastery learning, competency based testing, and the back to basics movement continue to push schools in a direction toward outmoded views of language, teaching, and learning and away from what theory and research in language learning show to be sound.

I have begun to realize that if we really want to make lasting improvement in our schools, then we have to think seriously about how teachers learn. Their role is central to the improvement of education. Yet, it seems that state departments of education, textbook publishers, the lay public, legislators, and judges have more to say about policy and practice than do classroom teachers. It is time schools and the wider public recognize that teachers—not federal or state agencies, local school boards, administrators, or even curriculum specialists—are the ultimate curriculum planners.

When the door is closed, "it is the teacher who makes (the) choices and who conducts and guides the whole learning enterprise in the classroom and, hence, is the ultimate curriculum planner" (Saylor, 1982, pp. 163-164). As Helgeson, Blosser, and Howe (1978) concluded in the Rand Corporation study, "The teacher is key. What science [or math or social studies or language] education will be for any one [child] for any one year will depend on what the child's teacher believes, knows, and does—and doesn't believe, doesn't know, and doesn't do" (p. 19), whether the teacher is a classroom teacher, a subject specialist, or a teacher educator. The quality of our own understandings about language, reading, writing, child growth and development, materials, and methods will to a large extent influence what we do in the classroom.

All of us, then, need to continue to find ways to be productive learners. John Dewey said that the best way for teachers to learn more about teaching and learning is to step back and reflect on their own experiences. In his view, to do otherwise was to become stagnant and dependent on external decisions and outside authority (Perrone, 1978).

So I accepted the challenge of this topic, and, engaged in a case study of one, I reflected on how I learn as a teacher. Each time I had an "ah ha!" experience, I would ask myself: "What did I learn? What did I do? Where did it happen? Who was involved? What happened next?"

Personal Experience

Let me tell you about one of my experiences. At a conference, I was listening to Martha King talk about children's language development. Near the end of the speech, she argued that it was time we changed the way we think about the language arts. She said the language arts should be reformed on the basis of the functions of language and not around the four traditional categories of speaking, listening, reading, and writing. She argued that if we want students to become effective language users who are skilled at talking, reading, and writing for many purposes, then we have to pay more attention to how context affects language use. We should concentrate less on the mode of discourse, such as narrative or expository writing, and more on the field and the tenor of the discourse in the classroom. She gave examples from actual classrooms that vividly illustrated her point. When King finished, I thought, "Of course, it all makes sense!"

About a year before I heard King speak, I read Halliday's *Language as Social Semiotic* (1978), in which he wrote several essays about how context influences the way language is used. In these essays, Halliday argued that the field, mode, and tenor of discourse are so entwined that we must understand these concepts if we want to understand why people use language as they do in a particular situation. Halliday is a linguist; I am not. Although some of his work is not easy to understand, I knew intuitively that what he was saying about language had important implications for education. However, I was not sure how to relate his ideas to classroom teaching.

So I read other theorists, people who were dealing with the same concepts but talking about them in other ways. With each new reading, I had a better grasp of what Halliday meant by field, tenor, and mode and how these concepts help to explain not only oral language, but writing and reading as well.

Several months later, I was working with colleagues on a research proposal, and we were studying the influence of literature on students' narrative writing. We wanted to look at the content, structure, and language of their writing to see if we could find connections to the materials they read and the instruction they received. I drew some interlocking circles to illustrate the relations among the three components of writing, and my colleagues and I started to brainstorm some of the features of interest to us.

Suddenly I said, "I've got it!" I began to scribble notes on the diagram (see Figure 1) and explained, "When we look at the content or ideational component of their pieces—the people and events, the ideas and feelings they write about—we're dealing with the field of discourse. We can say something about the range of subject matter students address in their writing and the source of that content. Is it personal experience, television, literature, other curriculum activities, or teacher assigned topics? From the structure of the texts, we can describe the forms or modes of discourse students use in writing stories and make inferences about their exposure to and knowledge of various genres and genre conventions. When we look at the language features or wording, we're really dealing with the interpersonal component of the writing, and we can say something about the tenor of the discourse, the style and mood, and the way kids relate to their audience and put voice into their pieces."

I was excited; I was making connections. I thought I saw how we could use Halliday's concepts to describe the rhetorical context as well as the features of children's writing. From their initial reactions, I knew that my colleagues were confused about what I meant and had no idea why I was so excited. They were looking at narrative writing from a literary point of view; I was looking at it as language in use. But they indulged me, asked questions, and challenged me with "What about this?" and "What about that?"

Trying to explain what I meant helped me to clarify my own thinking and to understand why I had had difficulty with Halliday's theory of language. I thought of mode, field, and tenor as terms that

Figure 1
Some Thoughts on
Ways to Look at Children's Writing

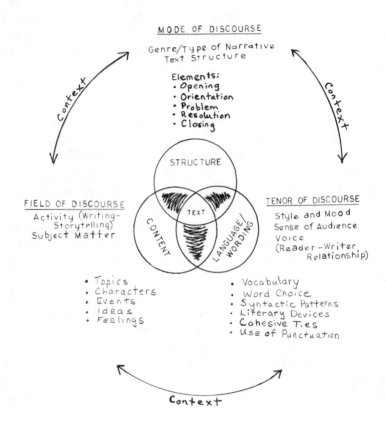

referred to the actual components of a spoken or written text, and he was using them to describe the social/situational factors that determine how text is created and interpreted—a subtle but important difference.

It was not until after I heard Martha King's talk that I saw clearly how these concepts apply to language use and instruction in the classroom and thought of ways to use them in my own teaching. She spoke my language and used classroom examples I could relate to. She had advised us to alter the role relationships among students and between students and teacher (vary the way they work together) and change the field (let students select the topics and activities) and see how the tenor and mode (forms and functions of language) also change.

I decided to test this hypothesis in my undergraduate course on Language and Literacy. I usually specify kid watching activities for students to try, related to the focus of each session. They select one activity and gather data to be discussed in class. I changed the approach and asked students to decide what data they wanted to collect for the next session. We had been exploring the relationship between language and cognitive development, and they decided to try one of the activities in *Children's Language and Learning* (Lindfors, 1980, p. 272). They observed in classrooms and wrote down the first ten questions they heard children ask.

When we met, I asked them how they wanted to proceed. They chose to discuss their findings according to the grade levels they had observed. When they were in groups, I left the room to see what would happen if I were not present during the discussion. As I stepped outside into the reception area, my secretary asked what I was doing, knowing I had a class. I said, in a half joking manner, "I'm teaching." "Why do you look so nervous?" she asked. I *was* nervous, not knowing how this experiment would turn out.

Given the volume of interaction when I returned an hour later (we have three-hour sessions) and the nature of the group reports, it was obvious that these education students were using language in different ways and for a wider variety of purposes than usual. It was clear that they had dealt with ideas in depth and had raised important questions about the procedures they used to collect their data and the meaning of their findings. I learned that my students need more time to interact among themselves (without me) so they can grapple with new ideas on their own terms.

I realized that, even in our teacher education courses, where we try hard to use an informal approach, most students perceive us as the "teacher" and the "authority," not as collaborators in the learning process. More than twelve years of schooling have taught them these assumptions. Why should they believe a college classroom is any different?

When we talked about the session, it was obvious the students were aware of differences in the way they interacted with one another when I wasn't listening and joining the discussions, as I usually do. We talked about how the context of the situation varied from other sessions and how the form and tenor of the discourse had changed. They talked about implications for their own teaching, and I had a better understanding of what Halliday and King were talking about.

Sources of Knowledge and Ways of Learning

As I reflected on this experience and others, I began to identify characteristics of my own learning. I was hesitant about making generalizations from only my own experiences, however, so I talked with several of my colleagues and with teachers trying to implement new ideas in their classrooms — such as a process approach to writing, big books, and a literature based reading program. I asked them to think about how they learn, to describe changes they had made in their own practices, to explain why they had made these changes, and where they had found the ideas.

I discovered that their sources of new knowledge and ways of learning were similar to my own. These are shown in Figure 2.

Theory and Research. Important sources of new knowledge are theory and research. In the past twenty years, we have learned much about language and language learning. Researchers from a range of disciplines — psychology, education, reading, psycholinguistics, sociolinguistics — have had a significant impact on the way we view language, reading, and writing. Their findings are exciting and have important implications for instruction at all levels. Teachers who are familiar with recent theory and research also find them exciting and valuable sources of information about children's language and literacy development.

As sources of knowledge, theory and research are important because they supply us with concepts and ideas we can use as guides

Figure 2
Sources of Knowledge – Ways of Learning

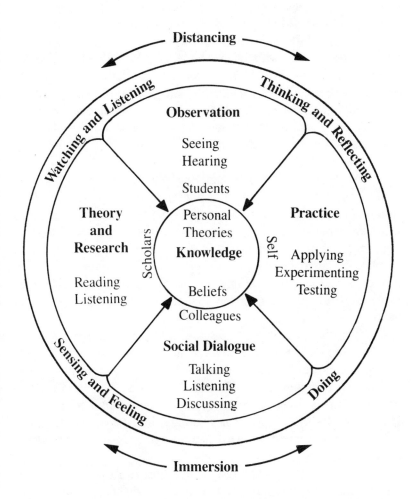

in observing and interpreting students' language behavior. They also provide valuable suggestions about conditions and activities that facilitate continued growth and learning. As an example, think about how Martha King used Halliday's theory to suggest needed changes in practice, which I in turn tried in my classroom.

As I have said elsewhere (Jaggar, 1985), no specific theory or research study or curriculum guide can prescribe what is appropriate for individual students in a particular classroom. Only teachers can make those decisions. Formal theories and the research on which they are based are descriptive, not prescriptive; they provide possibilities, not formulas for practice.

Knowing the research is valuable, because it provides a background of ideas against which we can compare our own knowledge and experiences. If the ideas make sense – given what we know about children, language, teaching, and learning – we can use them to refine our practices. If they don't, we may think of other interpretations that will help us to clarify the reasons behind our instructional choices (Barr, D'Arcy, & Healey, 1982, p. ii).

We often mistakenly assume that good teaching is simply a matter of knowing the research or putting theory into practice. The trouble with this notion is that knowing what research or theory *says* is not the same as knowing what it *means*. For research and theory to be meaningful to teachers and teacher educators, we must be able to relate the language and ideas to personal theories woven from our own past experiences. Learning involves connecting new ideas and experiences to old ones in a way that allows us to give meaning to the new.

One teacher I interviewed said it well: "While I was teaching, I became more and more convinced that reading could be taught through literature. I had been raised on literature, and it had worked for me, so I thought it would work for others. My beliefs were grounded in my own experiences. So when I found people like Holdaway (1979), I learned new things, but it was like coming home....It was something that I had always believed, so his ideas made sense."

Practice. Theory and research are just two sources of information teachers can use to enrich their knowledge base. Knowledge is also gained through practice and through our own teaching experiences. John Dewey said that "we learn by doing." We all need opportunities to try new ideas to see if they work. I *knew about* field, tenor, and mode from reading Halliday and listening to others, but it was only when I tried to apply the concepts in analyzing children's writing and in my own teaching that they became useful. Now I *know how* to put the knowledge to work.

Not only did I learn from the experience, but my students learned also. They became aware of how the social situation influences how they use language, and they began to think and talk about ways to apply this new knowledge in their own teaching. Based on their experiences, they were constructing their own theories about how context affects language use in the classroom.

Experience alone is not enough, however. As Amarel (1980, p. 5) says, "experience provides only the raw material for thought; it will not in itself nourish teaching practice." In discussing professional growth and development, Posner (1985, p. 19) reminds us it was John Dewey who argued, "we do not actually learn from experience as much as we learn from reflecting on that experience." Reflection, turning a subject over in the mind and giving it serious consideration, frees us from routine activity and dependence on outside authority and enables us to act in a deliberate and intentional fashion to accomplish what we want to do.

"Reflective thinking," says Posner, "allows the teacher to examine critically the assumptions that schools make about what can count as acceptable goals and methods, problems and solutions. Although we all must live within some constraints, often we accept as predetermined by authority or tradition far more than is necessary" (p. 20).

Posner goes on to assert that there is a constant interplay between choice and constraint in teaching. "Teachers, as professionals working within a powerful institution, have the opportunity to shape their identity, to take a stand even when in conflict with others, and to question common practices" (p. 22).

Observation. We also can learn from being skilled observers. The key to effective teaching is building on what students already know. The best way to discover their knowledge base is to listen and watch closely as they use both spoken and written language in a variety of settings and circumstances. Careful observations will reveal students' special interests, styles of learning, and patterns of language use. As we reflect on the emerging patterns and compare the new information with past observations and with our knowledge of language development, we can better determine what our students know and can do with language.

As Amarel (1980, p. 5) points out, "The teacher as observer is, in fact, the teacher as learner, who shares a context for learning with the student—a context in which the specifics of what is learned will vary for each one." Amarel adds: "This portrait of the teacher as learner, as an active decision maker, who uses information from the flux of classroom life to fashion her instruction, is not a common one. It suggests, for example, that it is not sufficient for a first grade teacher to know in a general way how six year olds behave or what skills...they can be expected to possess; that educational goals prescribed at the state or district level do not constitute a sufficient basis for planning and guiding the instruction of particular children. This conception of teaching achieves integrity only when paralleled by a congruent conception of the nature of children and how they learn" (p. 6).

Observing students in the classroom and other settings (such as the playground and cafeteria) can tell us things about their language and learning that we can discover in no other way. Observation is critical to good teaching. When observation is combined with informed reflection, it becomes inquiry, that is, careful study that leads to sound judgments about students and to continual learning for teachers.

Social Dialogue. Dialogue is essential for professional development. Just as we learn through reading, we learn through talking. Talking about research, theory, or practice permits us to examine our theories and beliefs and helps to clarify our thinking. Making our ideas explicit through discussion can lead to a fuller understanding of things that we had previously known only intuitively. "Moreover, language makes it possible for us to think about what we know and to take conscious responsibility for it, reshaping it for new purposes and taking a critical attitude to it" (Barnes, 1978, p. 156).

My richest learning experiences have been in collaboration with colleagues. Our discussions are exciting because we bring different perspectives to the study of children's language. But what is most important for us as learners is that we have a forum for sharing ideas and making connections between new and old ideas.

My experiences are in stark contrast to what Goodlad and Klein (1970) found in the schools twenty years ago, and, from all reports, the situation has not changed. They said, "It would appear that teachers are very much alone in their work. It is not just a matter of being alone, *all* alone with children in a classroom cell, although this is a significant part of their aloneness. Rather, it is the feeling—and in large measure the actuality—of not being supported by someone who knows about their work, is sympathetic to it, wants to help and, indeed, does help" (p. 94).

Teachers can help one another to grow, learn, and change through honest, professional dialogue, during which they talk, listen, and challenge one another's ideas in an atmosphere of respect and support. Britton (1982) said in declaring the '80s the decade of the teacher: "There are great opportunities for us, provided that we see that interactive learning applies to teachers as well as to those we teach; provided we see our role as helping each other to theorize from our own experience, and build our own rationale and convictions. For it is only when we are theorizing from our own experiences that we can, selectively, take and use other people's theories" (p. 214).

To summarize, when I reflected on my own experiences I found that

- I learn from scholars, researchers, and theorists in different fields, but also from interactions with my colleagues and my students. I also learn on my own through experiences I have in and out of the classroom.
- Language is central to all my learning. I read, I listen, I write, I talk to others and, as you can see, I draw diagrams to represent visually the ideas I'm struggling with.
- In the process, I learn in different ways. At times I feel the need to stand back and watch others. Sometimes I need to reflect on what I see, hear, or read. At other times, I need to immerse myself in activity, trying things out before I'm certain they will work. I can take these risks because I work in an environment where I have the freedom to experiment with new ideas and to make mistakes—where I have the freedom to learn.

What Are the Implications?

We must recognize that learning takes place from the inside out, not the outside in. Neither teachers nor those they teach change simply by giving them information, by being told about theory and research or new approaches. Unfortunately, we often equate knowledge with information. Language and literacy instruction won't improve in our schools if we continue to hold onto the idea that all teachers need is more information and everything will get better. Information is necessary, but it is not a sufficient condition for change. Let me give you an example.

A colleague and I recently surveyed a large number of teachers in New York and Texas about their concepts of reading and their beliefs about reading instruction (Greenlaw & Jaggar, in press). As part of the survey, we asked background questions about the reading courses they had taken, their approach to reading instruction, the materials they used, and their methods of diagnosing student needs.

The study yielded both good news and bad news for proponents of children's literature. The good news is that 75 percent of the teachers said they had taken at least one course in children's literature. The bad news is that over 60 percent said they never or only rarely use children's literature in teaching reading. They use basal readers and workbooks. The good news is that all had taken courses in the teaching of reading, and many had taken advanced courses in theories of reading and reading as a psycholinguistic process. The bad news is that 78 percent reported that they don't use miscue analysis for diagnosis; they use standardized tests instead.

To grow and develop, as well as to help their students learn, teachers need what all learners need, a climate for learning built on what we know about the process.

1. Teachers need time—time to observe students and one another, and time to read, think about, and discuss new ideas from theory and research in order to determine what they mean for curriculum and instruction. Learning is a gradual process. It involves changing what we believe, how we think, and what we do in the classroom. Everyone I interviewed said that it takes time to under-

stand new concepts and make them their own, whether it's schema, miscues, invented spelling, the functions of language, or Halliday's concepts of the field, mode, and tenor of discourse. Change takes time and energy. It does not take place overnight, or as the result of a one day workshop at the beginning of the school year—a limited and common approach to staff development. Professional growth and development should be an ongoing process that is an integral part of the life of a school.

2. Teachers need the freedom to take risks and to experiment with new ideas, materials, techniques, and approaches. Learning is a constructive process. Knowledge is not something that exists outside the knower; it is constructed within by the learner. Genuine learning involves action and discovery. As Bruner and others point out, the key condition for discovery is control. The more we control and initiate our own learning, the more likely we are to acquire new knowledge and skills.

3. Learning is a social process. Teachers need opportunities to collaborate with colleagues and other professionals on new projects and to develop solutions to common problems. They also need real support and assistance—not evaluation and judgment—from administrators, supervisors, and curriculum specialists who know and care about what teachers are trying to do and who can provide informed suggestions about how they might improve.

4. Most important, teachers need a work environment that is conducive to reflective thinking and that encourages dialogue among professionals who are given the power to act upon their own decisions as curriculum planners (Glickman, 1985).

In this chapter, I have presented many pages of writing to describe the teacher as a learner. A Chinese proverb says it in three lines:

Tell me, I Forget
Show me, I Remember
Involve me, I Understand

I would add:

Trust me, I'll Learn.

Integrating the Curriculum for Teacher Preparation

Education Today

T his is a difficult time for those of us in teacher education. Never have public school practices in the majority of our schools been so far removed from what we know to be true about children's learning, particularly their language acquisition and reading and writing behaviors. Social and political pressures are pushing education in the opposite direction from positions indicated by current research on children's language and literacy learning. Researchers are presenting children as competent learners, actively engaged in discovering the structure of language, self-programing the simple rules of spelling, developing a sense of story, and seeking meaning in their reading. But the back to the basics movement and its ally, competency testing, have taken us back to the outmoded model of teaching that views children as empty containers to be filled with predetermined facts, which later will be spewed forth on standardized tests.

Where does that leave those of us who believe differently?

- At odds with many of the practices in our public schools today
- In conflict with many of the texts, teachers' manuals, and workbooks used in the schools

- With the recognition that our schools have failed to teach children as adequately as they could, but not for the reasons given by the press and public
- In the difficult position of teaching teachers who are frequently afraid to make any changes in their practices for fear their children's test scores will decline

We attend conferences, meet with other professionals who believe the way we do, hear about new research that supports our point of view, and return home determined to make a difference—but we are not quite certain how.

Theory and Practice

Theory informs practice no less than practice informs theory. It is obvious that if research is going to have an impact, it must become a part of the content of courses in teacher education at both the preservice and inservice levels of teaching. But this inclusion is not enough. As we planned our alternative teacher education programs at The Ohio State University, we realized that it was necessary to change both the content and our methods of teaching at the university level if we expected to create changes in the ways teachers were teaching.

We further asked ourselves how many of the principles that we knew to be true for teaching young children also applied to teaching teachers? While it may be dangerous to extrapolate from research with students from elementary school to college, it appeared to us that there were many connections between good teaching at the elementary level and good teaching at the university level. For many principles of teaching, we can draw parallel relationships that apply to both teaching children and teaching teachers. I will explore nine such relationships.

Integrated Teaching

We decry the fragmentary nature of teaching young children meaningless parts of words out of context, spelling without relationship to writing, and writing without relationship to real communication. So, too, do we find unacceptable the fragmentation of courses for teacher training. The research reported by Carol Chomsky, Courtney Cazden, Donald Graves, and others has shown the inter-relationship among reading, language, and exposure to literature. We need to model this belief and teach all three of these courses in an integrated academic setting. We need expertise and depth of un-derstanding in each of those disciplines, but we also need to help students see the relationships among them. In order to counteract the effects of many years of fragmented, passive listening, which characterized their previous schooling, education students need to experience whole, integrated teaching.

In our programs, students registered for one course in lan-guage arts, literature, and reading each quarter for credit. This ar-rangement provided for the academic technicalities. In fact, all three subjects were team taught for three quarters in one integrated course. We required a year long commitment from the students in order to combine the courses.

Time

Another obvious guiding principle is that real education and change both take time. If we are interested in the growth and gradual development of children's learning over at least one year, then shouldn't we have the same interest in the development of a teacher over a length of time? In the United States, we expect everything to happen yesterday. We look at products rather than persons — at scores on reading and achievement tests, final papers, and exams rather than the process of becoming a reader or a teacher.

We have more research on the process of learning to read than we have on the process of becoming a teacher. But those of us who teach in the quarter system know that it takes more than thirteen weeks to teach even an adequate course in children's literature, lan-guage arts, or reading. In the quarter system, we spend more energy on starting and stopping than on teaching and learning. Having the same students together as a class for a whole year is pure luxury. They get to know you and one another; you, in turn, know them as human beings in the process of becoming teachers, rather than as names on your computer printout sheet. Time, then, enables you to personalize teaching, to individualize teaching in terms of students' needs, and to help them grow in the process of becoming teachers.

Both the graduate program and the undergraduate program were three quarters (an academic year) in length. The undergraduate or EPIC program included methods courses and student teaching and took almost the complete time of these juniors in education. The graduate program involved one course each quarter, plus four full Saturdays for each of two quarters for workshops, trips, and other hands on experiences. All courses were team taught by the same group of professors and teaching associates, with one team for the graduate program and another serving the undergraduate.

Authentic Experiences

A third principle in planning these experimental teacher education programs comes from understanding children's need for authentic experiences. We know that children will learn the skills of reading, writing, and spelling when these skills are a part of the necessary context of learning that has power and importance for them. Reflection and self-evaluation need to be part of these authentic experiences and part of all teaching. These principles are equally true for undergraduates and teachers.

Each year, we have begun the undergraduate program with an overnight experience in Barnebey Woods, a large tract of woods and stream owned by the university. Here the students come to walk, explore, write "thought ramblings," and work in groups on nature projects and displays.

One assignment asked each student to find a nature specimen—a leaf, a rock, a flower, or an insect. Students then were asked to sketch or paint their object and to write a detailed description of it. In order to realize their own creative powers, they were asked to do something imaginative with the object; for example, be its voice, write a story or poem about it, or carry on an imaginary conversation with it.

After projects were presented and artwork carefully displayed with written observations and stories, students were asked to reflect on the experience both in their field trip booklets and in class. They were asked to consider these questions.

- What kinds of oral and written expressions grew out of the experience?
- What thinking processes did you have to go through to create what you did?
- What did you have to know to do what you did?
- What were the educational implications for such an experience?

Finally, students reflected on the total experience. We asked them if they could state the educational objectives we had for taking them on such a trip. Through this reflective process, implicit knowledge was made explicit.

Saturday workshops for the teachers included experiences such as cooking, making books, and engaging in sensory activities such as "blind walks." The teachers took trips along a busy street and taped sounds, surveyed bumper stickers, collected and categorized litter, and interviewed people. Those activities were intended to help teachers see and feel as a child, to recapture the excitement of learning for themselves, and to extend their visions of what makes dynamic learning.

We must remember that the teachers we are now teaching belong to the generation of TV raised children. They may have missed the sights and sounds of exploring an unknown territory or engaging in imaginative play. Rather, they may have spent much of their lives passively seated in front of television. How, then, can they open up the real world of learning, a world they may never have experienced, for their students?

How can teachers know what is involved in making leaf prints, mapping an insect's trail for ten minutes, making a game from a book, or constructing a chart comparing five versions of Cinderella, unless we give them the opportunity? By experiencing the activity, they can see the concentration involved, the opportunities for much focused talk and for writing and reading, and the learning potential. Telling them will not do; lecturing while they sit passively digesting our words of wisdom will never change their teaching styles. Doing may effect behavior change—provided they understand the reasons behind the doing.

Making Sense of Teaching

A fourth principle is that while it is important to plan enjoyable activities in classrooms, those activities must have additional goals for student learning. It is important for teachers to know the purposes for the learning activities they participate in and that they plan for their students.

It is almost a truism today to talk about children's search for meaning. We know as we observe and record their miscues in reading or their so called spelling mistakes that those errors are usually the result of children's attempts to make sense of the book or to communicate.

In a similar fashion, preservice and inservice teachers want to make sense of their teaching. Our goal for the experimental programs was to produce informed teachers, teachers who know why they taught as they did and who could explain it to others.

One of the requirements in the master's program was to read aloud to children at least once every day and preferably several times a day for kindergarten or primary grades. One of the teachers was concerned because her principal had visited her third grade twice while she was reading aloud and then had asked her to come in for a conference the next week. She knew he was going to question her reading aloud since she was the only third grade teacher who took time to share stories with her pupils. I asked her if she knew research that supports a read aloud program, and she immediately referred to studies by Chomsky, Cohen, Cullinan, Jaggar, and Strickland.

The teacher was ready for her conference, and when the principal asked why it was necessary to read to third graders, the teacher responded by quoting the appropriate research. At the next faculty meeting, the principal announced that all teachers should read aloud to their students at least fifteen minutes a day! Teachers need to know why they are doing what they are doing and be able to inform administrators, parents, and other teachers.

The Value of Talk

This same teacher had to justify the value of allowing her students to talk in the classroom, to work together to achieve their common purposes. Once again, she was able to draw on research. This time she gave her principal *From Communication to Curriculum* (Barnes, 1976), which shows how children frequently talk their way through to meaning and effective communication.

In most university classes, including those in education, we look to the professor as the fountainhead of all knowledge; the students are seen as the recipients. Yet, surely college students have much to be gained from talking together, not in sharing their ignorance, but in probing their knowledge or looking at various aspects of a particular subject.

In teaching children's literature, we frequently had in depth discussions of a book such as Molly Hunter's *A Stranger Came Ashore*. Rather than have the whole class discuss it, we might divide into small groups with different assignments. One group might find all the Scottish superstitions and talk about how the author used these to predict the action of the story. Another group might list all the clues they could find as to the identity of the Stranger, including who knew his true nature first. A third group might read Jane Yolen's picture book *The Greyling* and decide how they could link that with *A Stranger Came Ashore*, while yet another group might be looking for appropriate sea poems to capture the eerie mood of Hunter's book. After twenty minutes of focused talk, students had something to share with the entire class that could enrich everyone's interpretation of *A Stranger Came Ashore*. Another time, we may read different books linked by a common theme, such as survival, or investigate books by one author, such as Madeleine L'Engle or Betsy Byars, or books of a particular genre such as high fantasy.

In this way, students become acquainted with more books and a greater variety of books. They are developing an increasing sense of form and slowly beginning to develop a frame of reference for literature. Always, there is time for them to hear different interpretations of books and poems and learn that there is no one correct response; there are many different responses.

Teachers who are students in the university are not empty vessels; they can teach one another and they have much they can share, if only professors will take advantage of it. If we believe that in elementary schools there should be as much student talk as teacher talk, then inservice programs should allow for as much teacher talk as professor talk.

The Importance of Learning Skills in Context

We would all acknowledge that basic skills are important in teaching the elementary school child. Skills must be taught in a meaningful context, however. Then children see that such skills provide power to do what is important for them.

Certain basic skills of observation or kid watching are essential for teachers to know. These, too, should be taught in real classrooms with real children and meaningful materials. Our master's students were all asked to look at children's various responses to literature. They analyzed children's telling of stories to see what kind of a sense of story they had developed. They learned to give and interpret Clay's "Concepts about Print" test, and they evaluated children's writing samples over a period of time. They analyzed children's spelling to determine what children knew about spelling, and then looked at the errors. Teachers made miscue analyses of children's reading and then looked to the probable causes of those miscues.

Skills of observation and analysis were not taught once and then forgotten. They were introduced gradually in the beginning of the year by asking teachers to shadow a child for one day, to try to have a significant conversation with the child, to look at the child's response to a story, to evaluate a retelling of a story, and then to discuss what those behaviors told them about that child.

Throughout the year, other assignments sharpened the teachers' observation and evaluative skills. At the end of the year, teachers listed all the techniques they knew to help them learn about children. We emphasized how much more they would know about a child through the consistent use of these kid watching strategies and how much more than the results of a single test they could then share with parents.

Reinforcement of Learning

Reinforcement of learning is as essential at the university level as in the primary school. Just as children do not always understand a concept the first time they learn it, teachers, too, need reinforcement of their learning, particularly when methods cut across their traditional beliefs of what constitutes good teaching. For this reason, we believe it is essential that in our college teaching we model what we perceive as good teaching practices.

By team teaching, one of us could play the role of the observer and make explicit certain teaching practices that were being used. Otherwise, students became so caught up in the doing of a project that they could miss the implications for teaching. Analysis of the *process* of learning always took precedence over the *product* of learning.

We also were fortunate that over the years we produced teachers who were taught in this fashion, and they in turn have become superb models for student teachers. In these classrooms, the student teachers' educational philosophy and practice were reinforced rather than destroyed. Too often, student teaching becomes a kind of indoctrination into mediocrity as students are told, "Don't believe what they say at the university; this is the real world, and this is how you have to do it." The real world of teaching for our students, however, illuminated the philosophy and methods advocated by the university alternative program. Students could visit and participate in classrooms that modeled what they were being taught in their methods courses.

Recognition of Work Well Done

To be a good teacher it is essential to believe in the children's ability to do and learn and then to recognize and reward this learning. In teacher education, it is also essential to have high expectations for all students and then to be certain that they receive recognition when they are achieving. A former student told me that she has been teaching for seven years, and not once has a principal told her she was doing a good job. And she is a capable and intelligent teacher. Most teachers want to learn and to improve their teaching abilities. I abhor the use of the term "teacher proof" materials, for it implies low intelligence, lack of creativity, and no interest in individual children.

We have had teachers who could understand the implications of research for teaching but could never apply them in their own classrooms. In our master's program, we had one reading teacher who had done the same things with her students for years. That teacher began to read to her children, and she gave them opportunities to tell and write stories, because we had made such an assignment. Toward the end of the school year, her husband made a workbench for her classroom, and she couldn't believe the interest, the language, and the writing that grew out of the children's woodworking activities. We all celebrated her super idea! Slowly and surely, progress comes if you expect it and recognize it when it happens.

Continuous Support

Finally, we believe that such intense and personal education needs a support system even after students have received their degrees. Minicourses that carry only one hour of credit enable us to offer a brief in depth look at particular subjects or techniques of teaching. We have offered minicourses on Poetry, Picture Books, Folktales, Storytelling, Parents and Reading, and Observation Techniques. Each quarter, we try to bring at least one author or illustrator to campus for a lecture that is open to all; we have been fortunate to have many authors and illustrators visit our program. Teachers in the schools are always notified of the time and place of visiting artists and writers.

Another close link between the university and the field is the relationship between student teachers and their supervisors. Many of the supervising teachers have been former EPIC students or have been in the master's program. They know what to expect of the student teachers and work closely with the program.

We frequently invite one or two teachers to come to our classes to share what they are doing with literature and writing or, whenever possible, to take classes out to the schools to visit. It is absolutely vital to have teachers articulate what they are doing and why. The more frequently you can explain your program to others, the firmer becomes your understanding of the reasons why you are teaching the way you are. Teachers also need to hear from other teachers who really are teaching superbly. The more we can feature them, the better.

Another kind of support base we give to our teachers is to invite some of them to work on our quarterly periodical, which reviews new books in terms of children's responses to them. The WEB is unique in the field of reviewing because no other periodical regularly describes how books are used in the classroom. Recently, we have included a "teacher feature," which highlights teachers who work in a unique fashion or have a particularly outstanding program of literature and reading. Each issue of the WEB includes a web of possibilities based on a particular theme, such as folktales or books about houses, or a single book, suggesting activities and linking these with other useful titles. As teachers interact with other teachers in the development of these webs, some powerful learning and thinking takes place.

If I had to summarize my beliefs about teacher education, I would simply refer to it as the process of making connections between what we know about child growth and learning and practice in the school; between good teaching at the elementary level and good teaching at the university level; and between helping students and helping teachers grow in the process of becoming all that they can be.

Section Four

Change through Extending the Knowledge Base

Section Four Prelude

I t is not enough to have theories about what good education is. We can create school environments according to the directions of researchers and scholars, but those settings often are short lived. They change in response to the next set of researchers who visit. Real change must emerge from within the organization. The people involved must examine and change their own beliefs and theories; the organization must create within it a new culture in response to new knowledge.

Administrators and teachers who attempt to create new structures in schools make changes based on the best knowledge they have. They may draw from the research community, but they must provide the daily implementation themselves. To have integrity, implementation must be grounded in a particular setting or context. Those who are involved must do more than believe in the implementation; they must be able to evaluate it.

In this section, Monroe advocates an internal research program that tests programs and increases the knowledge base of those who implement them. As an administrator, he provides practical advice for combining research and inservice education. Pinnell conceptualizes change as a systemic effort within the educational setting and offers some suggestions for getting started. Watson and Stevenson tell a story about what teachers can do when they collaborate and support one another. Change is not seen here as a lonely struggle but as a dynamic process that gathers momentum as people talk with one another and engage in theory building. Goodman's conceptual framework acts as a summary for this volume and a challenge to the creators of educational settings.

Donald S. Monroe

Teacher Research and Decision Making: An Administrator's View

I f public schools are to be places where creative and intelligent people exercise their full range of ability, teachers, as well as university professors, must be given the opportunity to create knowledge related to teaching. Too often, people who enter teaching have a sense of being "acted on" rather than acting and see the teaching role as one in which the individual is poorly paid and over-managed. There are always the human rewards of working with children, but to attract and keep the most capable people, teaching also must include opportunities to exercise decision making and leadership skills.

One District's Plan

In our school district we have expanded and enriched professional roles so that our teachers are also researchers, authors, editors, and staff developers. Our actions grow out of a culture, or system of beliefs, that exists in our district. We see teaching as an unfinished business. We are dissatisfied with our own knowledge of teaching and learning. We look for intelligent, energetic people and then create a climate where they can exercise their ability to address our dissatisfaction and add to our knowledge. Finally, we reward creative activity through increased opportunities for professional visibility and leadership.

Our district always has been a place where people were thoughtful about their work and where professional activity and a high level of teacher participation were considered desirable. In the past few years, we have re-created and renewed this spirit of professionalism, and have engaged in activities that give this culture meaning and life.

Our own professional journal, *The Forum*, is written and edited by our teachers. Articles often report original research by district personnel. This journal is an important vehicle for sharing knowledge and for creating a self-image that suggests that we are interested in examining what we do and in adding to our own knowledge of our children and how they learn. This professional accountability is exemplified by the various kinds of studies we have conducted in our district. I would like to share several examples.

We were concerned about the teaching time devoted to cursive writing in second, third, and fourth grades. We wanted to help children express themselves in language and to learn writing and composing. We were concerned about detracting from real writing instruction by putting so much emphasis on cursive style handwriting. So we delayed cursive writing instruction until the fifth grade and subsequently performed a study of the handwriting of all sixth graders in our district and another district.

Neutral judges evaluated handwriting samples, and results indicated that the cursive handwriting of our students was significantly better than that of other students, even though our students had had only one year of instruction. At the same time, we compared attitudes of teachers toward the teaching of cursive writing and found that our teachers had more negative attitudes toward this activity. We concluded that in a fraction of the time, even with low teacher attitudes, we could accomplish the task of teaching cursive writing by waiting until the fifth grade. Teachers conducted and reported that research.

Another project was carried out by two fifth grade teachers who were frustrated with the way they were teaching vocabulary. They developed a dynamic new method that involved categorization and dramatization, and then they conducted a controlled study that compared the new techniques with traditional methods such as using lists of words, definitions, and testing. The dynamic method was significantly more successful. More interesting, it was more effective with lower achieving students than with higher achieving students. The teachers who conducted the study published articles about it and made presentations at national conferences.

A study team of ten, including teachers, a principal, and a school board member, has finished an examination of the question: "How has childhood changed?" We were contemplating a four year curriculum revision, but before we started, we wanted to know more about the future and about the kind of world our kids would live in. The study group looked at the literature and gathered their own experiences and observations to form some preliminary conclusions. They wrote to seventy school districts that had students with socioeconomic backgrounds similar to those of our students. They asked the superintendent to distribute to primary, junior high, and high school teachers some open ended questions concerning characteristics of children and aspects of their lives. After gathering the data, they found some patterns across the groups, and their findings have influenced the shaping of the curriculum in five surrounding districts.

One finding was that many children have a difficult time seeing a task through to completion. Changes in family life and other factors have resulted in children's lives being fragmented, and their relationships with adults often are inconsistent and temporary. One of the primary goals of our instructional program is to create opportunities for children to have a more consistent relationship with one adult. We are looking at multi-age groups as a way of having a teacher keep at least half of the same group for two years. We also are considering having a teacher of one grade keep a whole group intact and teach the next grade. In this way, they have a longer period of time to work things out with one another.

The study group found that children lack opportunities for cooperation because they are so often on their own, watching television or using the computer. They have learned to fend for themselves in the absence of consistent adult/child relationships. Yet, for the survival of our world, children need to learn more about interdependence and cooperation. We are trying to build into the curriculum ways to foster interdependence and cooperation.

We want staff members to have a chance to publish and be rewarded for their extra efforts. In addition to the journal, we have a professional growth fund that teachers themselves administer. While most districts give extra salary to teachers who receive additional training, we give it to them for research, writing, travel, and exercising leadership in the profession.

Summary

I believe that this kind of activity could take place in any school district. First, administrators have to foster a healthy respect for teachers as capable professionals and have to let them make important professional decisions. The superintendent needs to put the life of the school district into the hands of the principals and the teachers and then must rely on the recommendations that come out of those relationships. It might be easy to say that our district is affluent and that resources are needed to accomplish research activities, but money is not really the issue. *The Forum* costs $1,800 a year for printing, and we employ a retired teacher who edits it. An investment of $5,000 to $10,000 can have a huge impact on a district and offers a good starting point.

Good teaching is a spinoff of this high level of professional activity among the teachers. The kind of climate and culture that exits in a school district ought to model the kind of climate and culture that exists in a good classroom. The kind of respect you accord teachers as learners and growing professionals is the same kind of respect you hope a teacher will provide the children in the classroom. What goes on in the classroom grows out of what we think of teaching and of learning. In our district, we focus on learning, everyone's learning, from the school board to the children to the superintendent to the teachers. The more we learn and the more we learn about learning, the better we teach.

Using Research to Create
a Supportive Literacy Climate

Many different groups—teacher educators, school boards, principals, teachers, central office administrators, undergraduate students, parents—share important responsibilities in providing education for children. All hold literacy development as a primary goal, yet lack of trust and disagreement often are characteristic of their communications, perhaps because of their different perspectives. They read different literature and research reports, are involved in different activities, listen to different speeches, hire different consultants, and respond to different guidelines and authorities. Each group talks about school in a different way, and each has its own language for framing problems and defining goals. No wonder we have such difficulty creating and sustaining good education.

Putting Research into Practice

In order to make positive changes in literacy and language education, these disparate groups have to develop ways of communicating with one another and of putting their knowledge of research into action. This task may require them to compare different avenues of research and work to find a common ground. The different groups need to negotiate among themselves and eventually develop a shared language that crosses territories. Most important, they must develop systemic ways of putting research into action. Too often, teachers taking university courses have learned snippets of research and some new ideas only to find that they do not work (survive) in the school because the context is not responsive. Likewise, administrators and supervisors have tried top down interventions only to find resistance from those who must implement the programs.

Some of these difficulties arise because those who try innovations do not take into account that the school organization is an integrated and holistic system. They fail to realize that change in one part of the system requires changes and adjustments in every other part of the system. This process takes place within individuals, between individuals, and between parts of the organization. This chapter presents some arguments for systemic change efforts that consider the social/organizational climate and proposes some beginning steps toward building-level change.

Research has increased awareness of the significance of social context in language and literacy development. Classrooms and schools must become systems in which every component works together to support children's language learning. Sometimes we must make changes in education in order to create those systems, and successful change requires an awareness of the various structures, systems, and groups that operate in school organizations. We often are puzzled by the failure of some innovations to succeed. When that happens, it is often because we have not taken into account some of the serious differences in perspectives mentioned previously.

Here are two images that, taken together, illustrate a major problem in putting research into practice. The disparity represented here (the gap between teacher education and what teachers actually do) is only one of the problem areas that inhibits change in education.

> *Image 1.* A group of teachers is participating in an exciting two week course at a highly respected university. They hear presentations on how children learn to talk, read, and write. They learn new assessment strategies. They examine actual protocols of children's talking and writing. They view films and videotapes and discuss them. They get concrete, personal experience in writing, art, and drama so they can bet-

ter understand the integration of those activities and their language base. They read current research by respected authorities. They conclude that language is the center of the curriculum and that teachers must be able to observe and use children's language strengths in the teaching of reading and writing. They leave the workshop with great excitement, returning to their own schools committed to the idea that language learning does not take place in isolated bits but is most effective when children are allowed to read and write for their own purposes and when the focus is on meaning.

Image 2. We enter an elementary school in the same city. The halls are clean but bare with no papers or posters to clutter the blank walls. A sign tells visitors to go immediately to the office. Children walk silently through the halls in lines. Teachers' projected voices are heard as we walk by classrooms. We enter the cafeteria, where some children are having lunch, watched by a monitor who admonishes them (on a bullhorn) not to talk, although we notice that some furtively whisper to one another. We see some adults in the hall, but they do not acknowledge our presence. At the end of the hall, we see a teacher shouting at a group of boys to "get in the room."

We peek in one classroom door. Groups of children are engaged in several different activities. One group sits in a circle, reading aloud one at a time from thick books. As each child reads, others follow silently. When the reader hesitates, several other children shout out the correct word. Some children sit at desks, which are arranged in straight rows. They are finding *p* words on a workbook page. Still others copy from the board a sentence that reads, "Today is Wednesday."

We hear a hum from the classroom next door and go to investigate. Here, some children are working on a story map of a book called *Rosie's Walk*. They are planning where each figure will go and talking in normal conversational voices. Looking down the hall, we see several doors closed, and one person looks out a classroom door disapprovingly. We go to the office, where we see several boys sullenly waiting to see the assistant principal. We meet the principal and ask about the school. She proudly shows the graph on her wall showing that test scores have risen for the past year.

For several years, I have been conscious of great discrepancies between what is emphasized and taught in university settings and what seems to be learned and perpetuated in schools where the students become teachers. Some of my most depressing experiences have involved observing student teachers in the classrooms where my former students teach.

Negative experiences are not always the case, of course. There are many success stories. Yet, even the best teacher education students are overwhelmed by the school environment as they try to implement what they learned during a summer workshop. They think that the success they achieve with students does not show up when measured by the school board or principal. Those who succeed sometimes feel isolated from the rest of the staff and feel it is not worth it to be different. They may feel intimidated by materials or by curriculum sequences that they must complete. School boards and administrators sometimes find it hard to see the value of a language rich classroom. Many teachers feel that ideas supported by research are unrealistic in view of their own situations. Are those ideas unrealistic? Or are they simply being implemented in isolation by teachers who do not realize the interactive nature of the system in which they operate?

Good teacher education programs can increase teachers' knowledge and sometimes their skills but seldom prepare them to cope with organizational systems. We work against ourselves when we forget that the school is a social system. We increase teachers' knowledge but neglect to look at the context in which they must put theory into practice.

Here are some contrasting ideas, all of which may sound familiar. The first statement represents an assumption or concept that might be developed in a graduate course or inservice session. The opposite statements describe policies and practices that I have observed in many schools and that I believe to be widespread.

Assumption	Policies and Practices
1. Children develop language through interaction. They need many opportunities to talk to teachers and to one another.	• No talking is allowed in the cafeteria. • In a middle school, every student must leave the building by ten minutes after the final bell. • Teachers may leave the building with the students. • In the mornings, students may not enter the building until the bell rings. • Students have three to five minutes between classes. • Teachers' ability to have good discipline is judged by the quietness of the classroom.
2. Children need many opportunities to write for their own purposes, and their work should be read by many audiences.	• Fire regulations are interpreted to mean that no paper may be placed on the corridor or classroom walls, other than one bulletin board. • Rules must be posted on all bulletin boards throughout the building. • Students in grades one through three copy a story from the board every day; in fourth grade they begin to write with "story starters." • Only "A" papers are to be displayed. • Standard punishment for tardiness is to write "I will not be late to school" fifty times.
3. Children learn to read by reading and need many opportunities to behave like readers, that is, to read easy materials fluently while focusing on meaning.	• All children must complete the readiness program and know their sounds before they are given books to read. • Children must complete all workbook pages related to a story before reading the next story.

- Teachers must use the teachers' manual exactly as directed, skipping nothing, except, perhaps, the enrichment section.
- Reading for pleasure may be done after seatwork is completed.
- Children younger than grade three may not take books home.

4. Children need rich experiences with written language, including being read to and having access to a wide variety of books.

- The school library is to be locked unless a class is scheduled there.
- Field trips require permission forms to be submitted in triplicate at least two months prior to the trip. Teachers must use school buses which cost $50 per trip, and often only one trip is allowed per year.
- Teachers' schedules are crowded, and priority is placed on "getting in" four reading groups and all skills lessons.
- Teachers generally read aloud after recess to "settle children down."

5. Assessment must be diagnostic; it must show the child's strengths, what he or she already knows, and provide direction for instruction.

- Standardized test results for each school are published in the newspaper.
- New district policies require an increase in testing and monitoring.
- Letter grades must be given on all papers and in all subjects.

The preceding statements show positions that are taught and may even be espoused by students in university courses based on research. These are in direct contrast, however, to what is commonly practiced by those same graduate students in their roles as teachers and administrators. All of us must adjust to integrate belief systems and practice.

Like any other institutions or organizations, schools are not just groups of individuals. Each person and operation is inseparably linked. Language, including reading and writing, takes place within a social context that we usually think of as the classroom but that should be viewed as part of the organizational whole. What happens in one part of the structure influences processes and outcomes in other parts.

Although connections may not be obvious, many environmental factors influence the school's capacity to foster literacy. Policies intended to solve attendance, record keeping, and discipline problems, for example, can affect the literacy program and inhibit or enhance children's development of written language. If that is the case, we need to think carefully about all policies and make decisions based on predictions of their likely effect on literacy development.

We can think of the classroom and the school as a learning context in which the total physical environment and all actions and interactions "teach" literacy. We have evidence that in the family/home environment children learn from everything around them, even though very little direct instruction takes place. Think what children are likely to learn about talking, reading, and writing in a home where the following things happen.

- They see other people reading all the time.
- Adults read recipes, appliance manuals, road maps, and newspapers as a matter of course.
- There are books, newspapers, and magazines in every part of the house.
- Pencils and paper are always within easy reach.
- People read and write letters.
- People talk and try to understand and share meaning.
- Adults and children point out exciting and special things in their lives, whether they happen on the freeway, in the supermarket, or in the library,
- Parents read to children, and children read to parents with the focus on getting the meaning and enjoying the story.

How many of the above activities are paralleled in school? In the home discussed, children do not have formal instruction on book handling or knowing that letters are important. Literacy just permeates the atmosphere, the ethos, the climate; it is in the system.

If we want to make changes to promote language development and to foster literacy, we have to work systemically, creating in school a pervasive literary environment where everything that surrounds the child "teaches" talking and reading and writing in a meaningful way. This kind of environment is delivered by a policy climate that is consciously created to foster literacy at all levels.

The environment for literacy must be fostered at the classroom level, and many classroom teachers do create rich literacy environments. But how much more effective those classrooms would be (and how many more teachers would work toward such classrooms) if, throughout the school, children met evidence that they are important; that their language is important; and that reading and writing are useful, enjoyable, possible, learnable, and worth learning. Much of our important knowledge was gained without awareness while we focused on something else. Can you remember learning that those black squiggles carried the message when you read? Perhaps someone taught you, but more than likely you learned it as you looked at and were read picture books.

Some changes can work to promote literacy development; others can inhibit it. If our priority is truly to teach children to read and write, we must think about the possible impact on literacy for every decision we make in schools.

Policy decisions are made at many levels: classroom, school building, district, state, and national. Those at the building and classroom levels seem almost trivial, yet everyday decisions may have the greatest impact on literacy. Whether we realize it or not, our policies are teaching children about themselves, about learning, about what schools value, and about reading and writing. What are students learning, for example, when the following things happen?

- Bells constantly interrupt reading.
- The intercom system takes precedence over everything else.

- Writing is done only for the teacher, who directs how most stories should begin.
- Reading is allowed after work is done.
- Reading time is largely devoted to filling in blanks or reading isolated words.

When students participate in narrow programs that deliver reading and writing as contained subjects to be taught only at specific times, children may be learning things that we did not intend to teach them.

- The only real reading is in reading class.
- You read only to learn to read better.
- Writing is hard and performed to please someone else.
- It's not a good idea to take a chance in reading or writing.
- Guessing isn't allowed.

All of the above attitudes can be subtly built through instructional programs and through everything else that happens to the child in school. In view of this, and guided by our knowledge of the child as a learner, we need to take a good look at what is happening in our schools.

At present, policymaking is usually done without conscious attention to a model of learning, although often a behavioral stimulus/response model is tacitly assumed. School staffs must begin to consciously devise policies consistent with new models of learning in that they create curricula that quietly and pervasively teach everyone that reading, talking, and writing are important.

Factors for Improving the Climate for Literacy

Creating such systems requires a holistic view of the school and a conscious attempt to change organizational factors that have an impact on literacy development. I am going to present some of the factors that I think need to be addressed if a school is to improve its climate for literacy.

The factors are organized as an inventory that can be used and modified as members of the school staff discuss their observations of the children they teach and as they learn more about children's development of language and literacy. The list includes descriptive statements to create images in the minds of teachers and other school staff as they envision what they want their school to be. These images eventually may guide all decisions, even those about everyday items such as seatwork. The list can be used by teachers and school staff to take inventory of their own school related to each item (Wayson et al., 1988).

This inventory can be used several ways. First, it can be used to assess school climate. Teachers may be pleased to find descriptions that are very true of their school. The inventory also will help identify some areas that might need work and will guide in targeting actions that will improve the literacy climate as a whole.

Another use of the inventory is to open communications so that perceptions can be shared. Staff members seldom talk about their goals and the problems they see in the school. One person might want to make available a wider variety of children's literature and display it attractively. Another might think that the school needs display boards for children's writing. Another might recognize that cafeteria workers and school clerks can help to promote literacy. All ideas might be feasible and could complement each other.

A rating of 0 indicates that the statement is not at all true of the school. A rating of 6 indicates that the statement is very true of the school. After completing the task, staff members can share their ratings and work together to determine strengths and needs and to begin an action plan to address priorities.

1. Working Together to Promote School Literacy

A 0 1 2 3 4 5 6 — Staff members work together to prevent failure and set children up for success in reading and writing. There is more emphasis on success than on failure.

B 0 1 2 3 4 5 6 — Teachers who are concerned about students' progress turn to colleagues for support, positive encouragement, and concrete help.

C 0 1 2 3 4 5 6   Adults in the school recognize their own responsibility to be sure every child learns to read and write regardless of home background or culture. Home background is not used as an excuse.

D 0 1 2 3 4 5 6   Adults in the school share a sense of direction and mutual purpose; they can describe goals and achievements with reference to the literacy curriculum.

2. Distribution of Authority and Status

Generally, fewer barriers to communication and action, more involvement in exercising authority, smaller status differences, and a broader concept of the professional role are related to a more responsive system and greater commitment on the part of staff and students. Achieving literacy requires participation by the whole school staff and by students.

A 0 1 2 3 4 5 6   Status differences that imply inferiority or superiority of one student or staff group over another are eliminated; grouping is critically examined.

B 0 1 2 3 4 5 6   Specialists in reading and/or language are seen as colleagues and team members in helping children learn to read and write.

C 0 1 2 3 4 5 6   All staff members realize that they have a role in helping children develop literacy and are responsible for setting examples that will communicate the importance of reading and writing.

D 0 1 2 3 4 5 6   Responsibilities and territories are shared and respected; people are not possessive, nor are they fearful that someone will take over their job, space, or materials. They say "our school" and "our students."

E 0 1 2 3 4 5 6   All staff members—including clerks, aides, and custodians—participate in faculty meetings.

3. Student Belongingness

As more students feel that the school serves them and their needs, treats them as valued individuals, and is a safe and happy place to be, the literacy environment will be enhanced.

A 0 1 2 3 4 5 6   Students know about and take an active, responsible role in the development of their own reading and writing abilities. Some choice is available in what they read and write.

B 0 1 2 3 4 5 6   Written and audiovisual materials—including what children read and hear read aloud—reflect the students' lives, families, community, culture, and language.

C 0 1 2 3 4 5 6   Students' work is displayed in classrooms, hallways, display cases, cafeterias, and other areas of the school.

D 0 1 2 3 4 5 6   Teachers and other staff know the names of students, not only those in their classrooms, but the others in the school.

E 0 1 2 3 4 5 6   Informal conversations take place between teachers and children to foster positive personal relationships.

4. Developing and Implementing Policies and Rules

Generally, when rules are made by the people involved and when expectations are clearly understood, the school is a more orderly and happy place to work. The more closely rules are derived from principles of learning and of normal human behavior, the more effective they are. Negative side effects may be prevented by evaluating rules for their possible effects on the climate for literacy.

A   0 1 2 3 4 5 6   Rules and expectations are closely defined, stated, and communicated so that people know what to do.

B   0 1 2 3 4 5 6   Disciplinary techniques are seen as part of teaching and are used to help children develop the independence and self-discipline they need to be successful.

C   0 1 2 3 4 5 6   Rules are not implemented when they clearly infringe upon the development of personal relationships between teachers and children, or between children and children, or when they inhibit the development of language.

D   0 1 2 3 4 5 6   Rules are not implemented in a way that deprives children of time to read or write.

E   0 1 2 3 4 5 6   Rules apply only to relevant behavior and not to matters that are trivial, highly personal, or have no effect upon the school, the class, or the child's ability to learn to read and write.

5. Curriculum and Instructional Practices

Practices that emphasize learning with content and processes appropriate for the students served, that provide diversity and choice in curriculum materials and activities, and that focus on the development of meaning in talking, reading, and writing are the best support for the development of literacy.

A 0 1 2 3 4 5 6   The curriculum for literacy is seen as more than materials and more than following sets of instructions as suggested in reading programs.

B 0 1 2 3 4 5 6   Individual differences and interests are respected and accommodated in the language/literacy instructional program.

C 0 1 2 3 4 5 6   Assessment strategies concentrate on finding out what the child knows and can do; much of the assessment is carried out within the whole acts of reading and writing.

D 0 1 2 3 4 5 6   Teachers are able to choose the best methods and materials to achieve the goals of literacy.

E 0 1 2 3 4 5 6   Teachers use a variety of written materials, including literature, rather than follow a rigid scheme for teaching reading.

F 0 1 2 3 4 5 6   Children are encouraged to work together and to help one another with reading and writing tasks.

G 0 1 2 3 4 5 6   Each classroom has a library, and the school has a library. The libraries are constantly used by children and teachers, and children are allowed to take books home.

H 0 1 2 3 4 5 6   Field trips, outside speakers, classroom study centers, and special research projects are seen as ordinary teaching methods that teachers may use without extraordinary administrative procedures.

I 0 1 2 3 4 5 6 Teachers are fully responsible for assuring that every child learns to read and write, but not for following a particularly prescribed way of organizing the curriculum or the instruction.

J 0 1 2 3 4 5 6 Reading and writing instruction takes place everywhere in the school and within all subject areas.

6. Processes for Dealing with Personal Problems

Generally, practices that help people cope with their lives outside the school and with problems not directly related to school matters stimulate greater commitment to participate fully in the work of the school.

A 0 1 2 3 4 5 6 Adults and students recognize that even good teachers have problems.

B 0 1 2 3 4 5 6 If one person has a problem with another, he or she discusses it directly with that person.

C 0 1 2 3 4 5 6 All people in the school recognize and celebrate when one of them achieves something good in reading, writing, or any other area.

D 0 1 2 3 4 5 6 People help one another to become independent.

E 0 1 2 3 4 5 6 All school personnel admit to mistakes; mistakes are seen as natural learning experiences.

7. Relationships with Parents and the Community

More open relationships with parents and other community members result in better opportunities to help children develop literacy.

A 0 1 2 3 4 5 6 Teachers and other school personnel

see parents as important sources of information and agents in children's development of reading and writing.

B 0 1 2 3 4 5 6   Teachers communicate often with parents concerning children's progress and interests in reading.

C 0 1 2 3 4 5 6   Teachers and other school personnel frequently visit students' homes.

D 0 1 2 3 4 5 6   Institutions and organizations within the community are used to offer support to students' developing literacy; for example, to display children's work or to provide books.

E 0 1 2 3 4 5 6   Parents and communities are not blamed for children's lack of progress in becoming literate; instead, efforts are made to link children's own lives with reading and writing.

8. Physical Environment

Generally, the environment in which literacy development takes place provides a setting which is pleasant, is convenient for children and adults, and reflects the interests, culture, values, and activities of students. The more the school environment looks like a workshop, a library, a restaurant, or a conference center and the less like a prison, the greater the chance to foster literacy.

A 0 1 2 3 4 5 6   The school provides many places where children's work can be displayed.

B 0 1 2 3 4 5 6   A rich variety of books are displayed everywhere in the school, and they are easily accessible to children.

C 0 1 2 3 4 5 6   The school environment is well organized to permit maximum student independence and interaction.

D	0	1	2	3	4	5	6

Students and staff members are involved in cleaning and decorating the school, and they feel responsible for keeping it attractive.

E	0	1	2	3	4	5	6

There are places in the school where small groups of students can work without disturbing others.

F	0	1	2	3	4	5	6

The cafeteria has places where small groups can sit, eat, and talk quietly.

G	0	1	2	3	4	5	6

Adequate materials are available, and they are organized for easy access and cleanup.

H	0	1	2	3	4	5	6

Adults and students are able to analyze trouble areas in the environment and to make provisions to solve problems.

A Plan for Implementing Change

To effectively implement change, we recommend using an organizational approach in which change agents work at all levels of the system to address problems and introduce ideas. Our most successful effects as professors of education have come from working with teams of teachers and administrators. After assessing the climate, they create a plan for change and agree to try several strategies that support each other. For example, here is a starter plan that takes place at several levels.

The Classroom Level
- Resolve to read aloud at least twice every day.
- Make a positive, nonevaluative home visit to every child in the class.

The School Building Level
- Have teachers eat lunch with children and talk with them.
- Have the principal read to some children every day.
- Create a display area for a variety of children's work.

The School District Level

- Begin a teacher study group to prepare teachers for selecting their own reading and language arts materials.
- Send parents some descriptions of what they can expect to see their children doing at school.
- Create ways for children to take more books home.

For such a plan to succeed requires commitment on the part of the school staff. This commitment cannot be created by an outside person; it must be built from within. Here are some suggestions for supervisors, staff developers, university personnel, teachers, and administrators who want to work with school groups attempting to make important changes in language and literacy instruction. These suggestions are drawn from my own experience and from studies of change in organizations.

- Help teachers grow and understand learning processes by carefully observing the children they teach. Complex ideas cannot be understood without acting on them.
- Insist that the principal participate in any inservice sessions given for the staff.
- Find ways to recognize steps toward good practice and avoid being overly critical along the way. For example, if a school staff has agreed that teachers will eat with and talk to children at lunch one day a week, applaud the practice and wait a couple of days before criticizing the writing program. If teachers are enriching the reading program by using lots of little books, don't insist that they throw away all workbooks right away.
- Go into classrooms and work directly with children. Hear them read, read to them, take dictation, wash paint brushes, and pick up paper. Your participation shows how important the work of the classroom is.
- Do not waste time and breath fighting labels such as "assertive discipline" or "effective schools." Few know what these concepts mean anyway. Instead, concentrate on convincing people of better ways to define effectiveness and create truly effective literacy environments.

- Try to communicate theoretical ideas in ways teachers can apply to their own students. Don't eliminate theory in favor of collections of ideas. Instead, insist that everyone in the school talk about *why* they made their decisions.
- Assume that all people have good intentions, are doing what they think is best for children, and are acting in good faith on the best knowledge they have. Administrators and teachers' unions often are placed in an adversarial position rather than being given an opportunity to listen to one another.
- Practices such as rigid grading and promotion procedures, frequent use of standardized tests, and lockstep basal reading systems do not mean that a situation is hopeless. Look for ways to enrich the literacy program; try out one step at a time and help teachers talk about progress.
- Don't wait for everyone to be with you to implement some good ideas. A few staff members who are enthusiastic and continually invite others to join them can convince most of the rest of a school.
- Avoid the "one shot" inservice session (a forty-five minute after school lecture that takes place in the host library with several teachers sitting in study cubicles grading their papers). Instead, invest resources in long term efforts. Try to get school staffs to agree to at least three sessions with developmental tasks to be done between sessions.

Above all, don't expect change to happen overnight. Change is possible if we are persistent and willing to work with a group over a long period of time and if we are willing to change ourselves and our own ideas in the process.

Dorothy J. Watson
Margaret T. Stevenson

11

Teacher Support Groups: Why and How

Laura:

Do you remember Jeff? The child I told you about who wouldn't put pen to paper at the beginning of the year? Today he wrote a wonderful two page story about a dog who had magical powers (MJKL PRS). I was so excited with his story that I showed it to the other first grade teacher. Her reaction was, "For gosh sakes, why do we want kids to write when we can't even read what they've written?" I didn't protest, but returned to my desk only to find a memo announcing that the basal reader adoption committee had reached a decision: starting next week there would be a series of inservice workshops to introduce the new materials. Well, there went any chance for the workshop on poetry in children's literature that some of us had petitioned for! The day ended with a telephone message from a parent who wanted to talk about the lack of worksheets, workbooks, and phonics instruction in my class. When was her daughter being taught the basics?

A s is typical in a teacher support group, Laura shared the good news first and then poured out the discouraging and disabling problems she was encountering. What Laura received from the twenty nursery school through college teachers who surrounded her that evening was an authentic (I've lived through that one) response to both the good news and the bad. Their comments represent both surface responses ("What a pain having a parent react in such a way!") and substantive ideas.

> Laura, do you have copies of the children's work so you can show examples to parents when you talk to them?
>
> Sending letters home to parents on a regular basis seems to help me get across the reasons we do some nontraditional things in our classroom. I can give you copies of my letters if you want to see them.
>
> Is there any way you can invite the other first grade teacher to get involved in a whole language activity that doesn't scare her?

All of Laura's concerns were discussed, and during the break, the teachers/friends continued to offer the kind of support one professional might offer another.

Introduction

In most support groups, the membership is trying to escape from something potentially harmful (drugs, gambling, food). In teacher support groups, the members are trying to move toward or stay with something important—a commitment to a point of view about children and about how they learn language, learn by using language, and learn about language in all its forms.

Support Group Members

For more than ten years in Canada and the United States, teachers have been coming together in small and large groups to gain and give professional support for the development of language arts programs that are often referred to as whole language, student centered, meaning focused, or literature based. Group members are teachers who have begun to take notice of students and their work in new and totally positive ways. They are teachers who have become interested in the work of educational researchers and theorists who value both children and their language, and who work to support curriculum and instructional procedures that keep children, their language, and the curriculum whole. Support groups include teachers who are on the verge of burnout—dissatisfied with what and how they are asking their students to learn.

Support group membership cannot be described by conventional categories such as grades or groups taught, number of years in service, or whether they work in private or public schools. A group might be made up of special education teachers, teacher educators, regular classroom teachers, both public and private school teachers, ESL teachers, first year teachers, and teachers nearing retirement. Some groups include principals, supervisors, directors, and administrators of special programs (and members point out that they are also parents and taxpayers).

The unifying factor that makes the members a family of professionals is that they hold a holistic view of language and learning. They all believe that reading and writing are learned through students' active integration, not disintegration, of the systems of language. Within that basic belief, the teachers are sure to hold varying degrees of knowledge about language and language teaching/learning. It also is likely that some teachers within the group recently moved from a strong skills oriented literacy program and now are seeking guidance from others who have experience in whole language teaching. Others in the group feel secure with their practical theory and want to explore, research, extend, and share their experiences with others.

> Their backgrounds are diverse, but they are all intrigued by the new information about how children learn and use language. Many come from schools where the curriculum is shadowed by mandated basal readers, workbooks and standardized tests, rather than illuminated by the experience and knowledge of teachers, and the strengths and needs of children. These teachers see the danger in inappropriate, insensitive, expensive, and time consuming skills and drills, and have moved, or are trying to move, toward authentic writing, reading, speaking, and listening in their classroom. These teachers often find themselves in very lonely situations. In attempting to find encouragement for their theoretically better way, they gravitate toward other educators who are also reaching out (Watson & Bixby, 1985).

Why Support Groups?

Although many organizations exist that are professionally enhancing, such organizations cannot meet the needs of the teachers described above on an immediate and personal level. Teachers who are going through professional changes (whether the changes are described as moderate or transforming) also are going through personal changes. That seems to be the way it is with teachers. And if such is truly the case, there are few of us who can or want to "go it alone."

Even in Canada, where most teachers have freedom to use materials of their own choosing, where they are encouraged to make the best use of trade books, of environmental print, and of nonprint material—even in these positive settings—educators in change need support and encouragement. Implementing whole language programs based on what children know rather than on what they don't know, and based on real literature rather than on trivialized texts and simulated stories, requires knowledge about the reading and writing processes, the role of talk, and the concept of language across the curriculum. Using these programs means knowing how to observe learners, plan and keep records, continue using new information, turn responsibility over to students, and keep parents involved. In other words, even in the most professional settings, teachers need one another in order to stay informed and to remain on the cutting edge of knowledge and practice.

In varying degrees, those involved in professional change need to *receive* encouragement, approval, advice, and sound information about their new professional adventure. Later in the change process, it seems just as important to *give* encouragement, approval, advice, and sound information about professional adventures. For this reason and many others, teacher support groups such as Child Centred Experience Based Learning (CEL), Teachers Applying Whole Language (TAWL), Children and Whole Language (CAWL), and Support, Maintain, Implement Language Expression (SMILE) are flourishing and are making vital differences in the lives of educators and their students. Following are reasons why teachers are turning to one another for guidance and growth.

1. In new adventures, teachers must have collegial support— to share successes. Children's marvelous linguistic advances must

be shared with someone who will value and celebrate them. Sharing with parents is rewarding, but the acknowledgement of another professional can be even more gratifying.

2. In new adventures, teachers also must have collegial support—to share frustrations. It is inevitable that there will be setbacks. At this time, only someone who is living through or has lived through a similar experience can be of help.

3. A major purpose of the support groups is to educate, but not to indoctrinate. Although teachers hold certain convictions about language and learning, they understand that those convictions can be put to the test only in classrooms where real children are involved. The educational/professional process is ongoing; it is circular. Research, theories, assumptions, and the implications of these for curriculum and instruction are presented for consideration in the support group. Then they are confirmed or disproved in the reality of the classroom. This reality is brought back to the group of professionals to set the stage for more research, theories, and assumptions.

4. By sharing their best classroom practices, teachers can rethink, resee, and relive the principles that underlie their own activities. By offering their best theory, idea, teaching strategy, story, or poem to someone else to consider, teachers are sharing in the truest sense of the word and are reflecting on their own beliefs and practices. Interestingly enough, when teachers share their best, their suggestions often come back to them enhanced, highlighted, and sharpened.

5. Teachers need support for political action. Although most groups are not formed for political purposes, the topic of power inevitably arises. Knowledge translates into power, for as teachers learn about language and the language learning processes, many feel the need to take back control of the curriculum, the classroom, and schooling for themselves and their students. When this happens, teachers need the support and resources of other professionals.

6. Within the support group, there are teachers who are interested in disseminating information about the theory and practice of holistic language arts programs by conducting workshops, by writing materials, or by presenting at conferences. The members of

the organization itself become resource persons, presenters, and program developers.

There are other important reasons why educators seek out teacher support groups. And there are less appropriate motivations, also. Teachers who are jumping on the whole language bandwagon usually do not remain in a support group, nor do those who come to a meeting, daring someone to convince them to adopt a point of view to which they are basically opposed. Support groups are not for people who need to be talked into a model of language learning of which they basically disapprove. Likewise, members do not come to meetings in order to explain and defend a whole language point of view; they have enough experience doing that day in and day out. As one member put it, "I come to TAWL to keep steady, to get ideas, to enjoy other teachers and their students' work. Don't ask me to spend my evening trying to talk a teacher out of doing skills and drills—not at TAWL!"

Where and How to Organize

At the latest count, approximately 125 support groups exist in Canada and the United States. Often they exist where there is someone active in teacher education at a university. This will be discussed later.

To give an idea of the purpose and history of two active teacher support groups, a description of the groups in Edmonton, Alberta, and in Columbia, Missouri, follows.

Children and Whole Language (CAWL)
Edmonton, Alberta, Support Groups

When a two week summer session, attended by thirty elementary teachers, was completed in August 1980, the last thing on anyone's mind was the organization of a teacher support group that would be the incentive for eight similar groups. But that is what happened. The thirty Edmonton Public School teachers were excited about the ideas introduced to them by a member of a Winnipeg support group called Child Centred Experienced Based Learning (CEL). New friends were exchanging names of schools and phone numbers, planning to work together to prepare for the year ahead.

But soon questions were raised. How could they give one another the moral support and encouragement they needed once school was under way? How could they explain their program to colleagues, principals, and parents? What if it didn't work? Their knowledge base was shaky. How could they plan for their own professional development? All eyes turned to the workshop organizer, their language arts supervisor. That's how it started. The group began to meet once a month to exchange ideas for professional development and to plan and implement special projects. There are now eight groups meeting in various parts of Edmonton; the two most recent are a second language group and a junior high group.

What made the CAWL groups catch on? Why has the interest remained so high? Members believe it has to do with the following:

1. Teachers are in charge and see themselves as being their own experts. Teachers chair the sessions, set the agenda, and decide on the projects. When new groups are formed, it is at the specific request of interested teachers.

2. The teachers receive tangible support from the district language arts supervisor and other personnel. A language arts consultant meets regularly with each group. Twice a year, support group chairpersons meet with the language arts consultants and supervisor to discuss plans and projects. These meetings enable the chairpersons to meet one another and to see their group as part of a city network. It is important to know that there are other teachers who also are committed to programs that are in the best interest of children. Quality materials developed by teachers are illustrated and printed professionally and made available to all schools in the district. Two notable examples are *We're Still Learning to Read,* a booklet written by two teachers for parents of students in grades four, five, and six, and the booklet *Whole Language* that explains aspects of the approach.

3. Teachers from the support groups are recognized as leaders and often are asked to make presentations at conferences, at other schools on professional development days, and even to the Board of Trustees.

4. Professional development is highlighted. Whenever a guest speaker or workshop leader comes for the school district, a

supper meeting is arranged for support group members so they may hear and interact with the guest.

5. Support groups limit the number of members to fifteen or twenty so they can meet in their homes. Occasionally, groups meet at a school or in the Centre for Education, but they prefer an informal setting. The small number encourages total participation.

6. The group members are rejuvenated and inspired by being involved in projects and conferences. When teachers feel the need, a summer session is planned. One of the most ambitious projects is the Young Author's Conference held on a Saturday in the spring for 200 students in grades one through six from the fourteen schools represented by the CAWL group. The children choose from sessions having to do with storytelling, puppetry, and writing and illustrating for the district publication, *Magpie*. *Magpie* is devoted to children's writing, to interviewing, to writing radio scripts, and to using drama activities. Another conference on children's writing was presented for over one hundred parents.

Teachers Applying Whole Language (TAWL)
Columbia, Missouri, Support Group

In the summer of 1977, an elementary teacher and a junior high teacher took a course in which new information was presented about language and about children learning to read and write through all the language arts. For the first time in years, these teachers were professionally excited, and they wanted to put their new knowledge into use. Because they felt they wouldn't be able to go it alone, a group of six teachers met to share their enthusiasm and their problems.

Their first two meetings were spent in venting frustrations — complaining about the insensitivity of others who didn't hold their point of view. The teachers needed this outlet, but they quickly realized that if they were to facilitate their own professional growth, they must do it in the same way they facilitated their students' growth — by beginning with their strengths. Immediately, the six teachers began to share ideas and to discuss their problems constructively. Through the years, two guidelines have been met: share the best, and begin with the positive.

The group has grown from six to one hundred members, with about forty attending monthly meetings. Because of the size of the group, the meetings no longer are held in homes, but in the district's board of education office or in one member's school. For years the group did not have a formalized structure, but several years ago officers were elected and a board of directors formed.

Major projects include writing two books of language arts strategies, starting other TAWL groups, becoming politically active, and holding a Renewal Conference each fall. At the conference, a resource person speaks to a large general group and then works one day with TAWL members and special guests.

Some Things We've Learned

Talking with members of various teacher support groups, we hear certain ideas about their organizations mentioned regularly. Some of the ideas have to do with forming and maintaining groups in general; others have to do specifically with promoting their own professional change.

1. The organization of a group must be a cooperative effort on the part of all the people who want to be a part of it. Although many groups have been formed by a teacher educator who has the resources of a university available, it is not necessary to have someone in such a position. It is, however, necessary to have at least one person who will take the initiative for setting up dates and places for meetings and for sending out reminders. A show of life and activity is vital. One person can get things started, but others must assume such responsibilities as preparing a list of names, addresses, and phone numbers; writing a brief newsletter; making telephone calls; or preparing a box of recent publications that are loaned at the meetings. It should be clear what the duties are and who is handling them.

2. Most groups focus around sharing. This activity is most meaningful when it is organized, however loosely. For example, a group might plan to share ideas and materials about a particular theme, which is decided on a month ahead of time. Invite teachers to share an article, a book, a newspaper clipping, or their students' work. Some

teachers will share; some won't; some forget; some bring things, but for some reason (which should be investigated), some don't; nevertheless, the constant opportunity to share is powerful.

3. Two or three teachers may present a more formal program. Demonstrations by teachers and role playing are often very useful when dealing with certain strategies such as conferencing. Teachers who are doing classroom research or graduate students who have conducted research might be invited to present their findings. Time for group discussion should be provided no matter what the program.

4. An evening of small interest groups often is fruitful. Some teachers may want to talk about writing, others about poetry; some may be planning a conference; others may be outlining a book of strategies or compiling a list of concept books for primary children. Another group may be discussing assessment of professional growth.

5. When the group gets large, forming an advisory board that meets prior to the regular monthly meetings is a good move. Members of the board can handle the busy work, report their actions to the entire group, and save valuable time for sharing and study.

6. Ways need to be devised for getting copies of important and informative articles into the hands of members. Money for copying material can be collected and kept for that purpose, or each member might once during the year bring enough copies of an article for all members. Book boxes maintained by one of the members can be checked out for a month.

7. Undertaking major projects that require cooperative planning over a period of time is an excellent way of getting to know one another and of presenting whole language concepts to other professionals, parents, and legislators. Preparation of booklets for parents, writing and publishing instructional strategy books, or presenting a conference provide continuity and a real sense of accomplishment.

8. Socializing is important, and some time should be set aside for it at every meeting. A holiday party or an end of the year celebration provides opportunities to share in an informal way.

9. Concerning professional change, help members realize that:

- Change is exciting, but it also can be frustrating and discouraging. Internal resistance, rather than external resistance, may be the most draining and confusing. When teachers are rethinking their beliefs about children, curriculum, teaching, and learning, they need to be as patient with themselves as they are with students and colleagues. Self doubt, ambiguity, and uncertainty are part of the process of clarification and understanding.
- Not everyone will appreciate new efforts and new ideas. It is possible for teachers in support groups to unintentionally and inadvertently threaten, antagonize, or even frighten others. Often our enthusiasm and the labels and words we use (whole language, humanistic, risk free, invented spelling, kid watching) act as red flags. Study the effect that ideas, actions, and our language have on others. Avoid being the in group, excluding those who are not in the know.
- The lack of an immediate positive response is not outright rejection. Teachers must not be guilty of placing a chip on their shoulder and daring someone to knock it off, nor of jumping to the conclusion that their ideas will never be reviewed objectively or considered fairly.
- Not all teachers making professional changes have to tread one particular thorny path—the one we took. Teachers must be able to orchestrate their own development. Some teachers will want to plunge intrepidly into a whole language program, while others will move slowly and cautiously—testing, implementing, questioning, and clarifying every move. Teachers must work out their own meanings and moves.

Laura:

It seems years since our last meeting; so many things have happened. I guess the most important thing is that I tried some of the things you suggested. I redid Ann's letter to parents and sent it out. After that, I decided it was time I asked them to come in to talk about some of the things we are doing in the classroom instead of doing worksheets. When the parents arrived, you can be sure the room was "littered with literacy"—the kids' stories and poems everywhere! I talked with the parents about the benefits of their children reading real literature, and about functional spelling, and I showed them examples of students' stories collected over a year's time. I can't believe how much the parents loved getting solid information. I think Jeff's dad had tears in his eyes when he read his son's three chapter book *Tiny—The Dog with Magical Powers.* Thanks for your suggestions and encouragement.

And the other first grade teacher and I are making a collection of poetry that appeals to our students. I've brought our list to share with you tonight...."

12

Kenneth S. Goodman

Language Development: Issues, Insights, and Implementation

T o be born human is to be born with a potential for thinking, for knowing, for understanding, for interaction, for communicating, and for developing language. Human infants immediately begin to realize this potential by forming a schema for assimilating and accommodating the experiences they have with the world. With a universal human ability to think symbolically—that is, to let something symbolically represent something else—and a universal need to communicate, human societies and human infants universally develop language.

Only humans are capable of the level of interaction we achieve because only humans have language, and language is necessary for the full sharing of feelings, needs, wants, experiences, and insights. Language becomes the medium through which thoughts are shared, but it is also the medium of thinking and of learning. Through language, people may link their minds, pool their experiences, and form a social base for a shared life view. Language is both the product of a culture and the principal means by which the culture is created. According to Halliday (1969), as children develop language they learn how to mean as the society around them does.

Language is social as well as personal; it is learned in the process of its social use. Thus parents, caregivers, siblings, peers, and others with whom the developing infant interacts play vital roles in the infant's linguistic development. They are less teachers than essential communicative partners, less role models than respondents, less to be imitated than to be understanding and understood.

Nature, Nurture, and Social-Personal Invention

While all that I've said so far is not novel, it represents a necessary major shift in focus from behavioral views in which language is seen as something outside the child, somehow taught to the child, or learned through conditioning.

It also is a shift from an old view, recently revived, that language is not learned at all but is innate. In this view, language in some underlying and universal form is preprogramed into the human brain, needing only exposure to some real human language to be realized. Such a view stems from two sources.

The first is the amazing feat of language learning itself. Scholars are astounded by how quickly, how early, and with what ease language develops. It's too complicated to be learned by such young minds so easily and so well.

The second source stems from the rejection of the alternative behavioral explanations as totally inadequate to explain language learning. Developmental research and linguistic theory have demonstrated the complexity of human language learning and particularly of the development of implicit rules by which novel language can be created by the learner. Some scholars, in rejecting the behavioral language learning theory, could find no alternative so they assumed language to be innate.

But the innate view of language development is at best unproductive. It causes scholars to treat development as uninteresting. Why study something if it is innate and happens universally anyway? At worst the innate view leads to the neglect of the social and personal functions, circumstances, and contexts within which human language develops. If language is innate, the most that social and physical environmental factors can do is inhibit the innate development.

Language learning in the past has been reduced to nature (nativistic) or nurture (behavioral) views, neither of which can explain how or why language develops. The how and why of language development are inseparable in attempting to understand both oral and written language development.

While progress on understanding oral language development has surmounted the obstacles of these inadequate theories, understanding written language development has been considerably retarded by them until recently. Partly, this difference stems from the obvious, spontaneous, and universal development of oral language, evidence of which was too overt to be ignored, whether oral language was treated as behaviorally conditioned or natively endowed.

Written language development is more subtle and becomes fully evident at a later point, usually after children enter school. So behaviorists could argue that written language development required explicit, controlled exposure to be a carefully sequenced hierarchy of skills and subskills for its development. They could further argue that those who have more difficulty in learning literacy need even more highly structured skill instruction; the inability to learn to read and write through the skill instruction is used to argue for even more tightly controlled and sequenced instruction.

And nativists could argue that it is oral language for which humans are preprogramed. To them, written language is a secondary and abstract representation of oral language. It is thus not learned like language but requires "metalinguistic awareness" – that is, explicit knowledge of how language works – for its development. Their view is that oral language develops so easily because it is not learned but innate; written language is more difficult to develop because it is learned. To some nativists it is not surprising that written language is hard to learn; in fact, it is surprising that it isn't harder.

An old issue in philosophy and psychology is the difference between knowledge *of* something and knowledge *for* something. Confusion between these kinds of knowledge has troubled both research and instruction. There is a strong tendency to judge what people know or how well they've learned by what they can discuss explicitly and abstractly. We have tended to judge the language knowledge of children by what they can say about it rather than by what they can do with it. Sometimes we go so far as to think of the knowledge of language as prerequisite to its effective use. Linguistic awareness or metalinguistic awareness are terms used variably, as Dybdahl (1980) points out. But to some they are used to cover abstract ability to discuss how language works.

Sometimes schools are encouraged to "put learners in touch" with what they know about language, that is, to help them reach a point where they can analyze what they do when they use language. While children may find this interesting, it's hard to find a justification for it as an aid to learning either oral or written language. At best, encouraging pupils to think about what they're doing while they speak, write, read, or listen makes them self-conscious and distracts them from the meaning being communicated.

Perhaps we are misled by the fact that children ask questions and make comments about language as they are gaining control over it. Furthermore, the more proficient children are in the use of language, the more they tend to be able to talk about it, since they can draw on their own intuitive knowledge to support their conclusions. Neither of these obvious facts establishes that metalinguistic awareness is a cause for or prerequisite to language development. In fact, it is more likely that metalinguistic awareness is a by-product of language development.

Of course, those who regard written language as an abstract school task to be mastered will see knowledge of language as a logical prerequisite to its use. In doing so, however, they are falling into an old trap of believing that children must be taught the symbols, structure, and rules of written language before they can read and write. The only argument in that case will be over which is the true knowledge to teach. Yet all that we have learned about language development indicates the fallacy of the assumption that knowledge of form must precede use.

A personal-social invention view cannot support these distinctions between how oral and written language develop or the relative ease of their development. If language develops to meet universal personal and social needs, then written language development is simply an extension of that process. It comes when oral language is insufficient to meet the communicative needs of the individual and the society. Furthermore, children growing up in a literate society in which written language performs vital functions will begin at early ages to internalize these functions, to experiment with the use of written language to meet their own functional needs, and to gain control over the forms of written language. In short, they will begin to develop as readers and writers before they reach school age and without instruction.

The differences in pace and degree of oral and written language development are not so much in how and why each develops but between the functions, purposes, and contexts in which they are used.

Application of New Knowledge and New Theoretical Insights

New research evidence and theories have given us insight into language and language development to use in developing new criteria for building sound, effective instructional programs. Viewing language as social-personal invention puts the teaching and learning of literacy in a new light. It can now be seen as a natural extension of language learning. That makes it possible to think in terms of building on what children already know, working with them rather than at cross purposes to them. Literacy is neither something to be taught a piece at a time nor something hard and abstract, but simply another language form to use in the functional context of its use.

Perhaps the most important new insight on language development is the personal-social perspective itself. That enables us to put language development, receptive and productive, in social and situational context. It enables us to see that what is happening in speech acts as a series of transactions between speaker and listener within a social-cultural context. We then can focus on the speaker, listener, discourse or text, and context, but only in relationship to all of the other components. This same view can apply to written language, except that the reader and writer are seldom in one another's presence, and the situational context is less complete.

In this new perspective, we have been able to gain new insights into language by looking at its functions—what it does and what it is used for, and then relating both linguistic form and language development to those functions. Here's an illustration of how useful that has been.

Goodman

For some time, teachers have noticed the overwhelming tendency of school beginners to write using capital letters. It's been commonly assumed that this is the result of parents teaching children to write with capitals. But there is little evidence that parents do much overt teaching of writing, and the writing that parents produce and children observe is generally cursive.

How then do children learn to write using capitals? The answer is all around us. One important use of print is in the signs that label our stores and buildings, call attention to commercial messages and offerings, and guide and control us. Street signs and traffic signs are examples of the latter. Overwhelmingly, these signs are printed in capital letters. So children who use capital letters in their writing must be learning to do so through their interactions with print in their environment.

Environmental print is not the only written language children experience as they grow up in a literate society. They see books, newspapers, magazines, and print on television, and handwritten lists, notes, and letters. But environmental print is pervasive and serves an easily inferable function.

This example illustrates how we frequently must put aside what we thought we knew about language when we look at language in the context of its use. We've all learned the rules for capitalization in writing texts. These rules are verified in the wide range of texts we read: letters, newspapers, books, and stories. But the rules do not apply in the range of other uses of print, particularly the print that children most frequently encounter on packages, television, street corners, and billboards. In fact, the print that is most attractive and situationally made meaningful is likely to be in capital letters. That doesn't make the rules wrong. But it means that they do not apply to all written language contexts and functions.

The example also illustrates some important insights about children's written language development. Print is part of the social and physical world in which children in a literate society are growing up. Piaget (1969) demonstrated that children engage in transactions with their world, interpreting what they see, feel, hear, and otherwise experience. They form hypotheses about what things are for and how they work. They develop schemata for their interpretations and modify these schemata as they gain further insights.

Drawing on Piagetian concepts, Ferreiro and Teberosky (1979) demonstrated that children in a wide range of cultures and socioeconomic circumstances are treating print as a significant part of the physical world. They are generalizing about how print as a system works, what it's for, and which features are important.

Clay (1977), Goodman (1980), Harste, Burke, and Woodward (1984), and others have shown that most children have developed strong roots for literacy before they have any school experience. Goodman has found that children's awareness of the function of written language in representing meaning begins separately and at least as early as any knowledge of letter forms and names. Others have found uninstructed children using sophisticated rules for relating the spelling system to phonology, letter names, morphemic features, and orthographic features.

While these rules don't always work and don't always correspond to adult rules, they show the active minds of young language learners at work in developing written language, just as they are in developing oral language. They show children learning the form of language as they try to use it functionally.

The example of children's early use of capitals is, of course, relatively trivial compared with many things that our new perspectives have made it possible to understand and appreciate about children's oral and written language development. What's most important about these new insights is that they are virtually universal beginnings of reading and writing among children in literate societies. Written language is developmental, very much as oral language is. Children are well on their way to literacy before they enter school. What we do to help them expand and build on what they've begun becomes the crucial issue.

We are redefining, in the context of this developmental view of how children become literate, what effective teaching must be. We have come to see teaching as supporting the learning, not controlling or necessarily causing it.

Much past research on effective teaching was focused on whether Method A or Method B produced the most learning judged by pupils' gains in scores on achievement tests. Such research was virtually useless since it was not likely to be rooted in any theory of language development or coherent view of what the pupils were learning.

Other research dealt with ways of teaching specific skills, often under controlled laboratory conditions. Such research was even less useful since neither the skill learned nor the laboratory conditions could be easily or meaningfully related to what happens with real language users reading, writing, speaking, or listening in real classrooms.

Now techniques borrowed and adapted from ethnography are being applied to the classroom. Researchers, operating from a theoretical perspective, are carefully monitoring what teachers are doing in classrooms as they interact with pupils. Often the teachers are part of the research team, verifying the observations and their interpretations. Now we can see the interrelationships of teaching and learning at the points where they are happening.

The research of Goodman (Allen & Watson, 1976) and others analyzing the miscues of readers has provided insights into the reading process and how it develops. The work of Graves (1975) and others has provided similar insights into writing development. We can begin to relate these research based theoretical perspectives of reading and writing to what we are learning about how teaching can support learning.

As important as they are, research and theory on language processes and language development do not translate directly into curriculum and instructional strategies and methodology. They provide foundational knowledge upon which educators—using their knowledge of children, learning, and curriculum—can build sound and effective practice. Educationists must decide the value of knowledge to curriculum and methodology. New curricula must grow from the integration of new knowledge about process and development with sound pedagogical theory.

We cannot afford to wait for all the returns to be in. There is a tendency for teachers, administrators, and curriculum specialists to throw up their hands at the unsettled and unsettling nature of the state of knowledge of language and language development. These are dynamic fields with conflicting schools of thought and new theories overturning old. It can be more comfortable for practitioners to sit on the sidelines and wait for the dust to settle. But too much is being learned to be ignored. We owe it to our pupils to utilize the best educational practice possible. If we wait for consensus, we will be staying with increasingly outmoded practice.

Furthermore, there must be two way communication between the practitioners, who have knowledge of the realities of teaching and learning in real classroom circumstances, and the researchers and theoreticians. In fact, we need interdisciplinary teams composed of academic scholars, researchers, integrators, disseminators, and practitioners who can make new insights available to teachers and learners. Such cooperation depends on mutual respect, particularly respect of teachers by the others. Teachers have the reality based insights that can turn new knowledge into effective practice. They can use the knowledge to monitor their pupils' progress, to plan instruction, and to evaluate and modify their own teaching.

The Battle to Apply What We Are Learning

The implications of our growing insights into oral and written language development for educational practice are already profound. We know so much about how and why children learn both forms of language, about the conditions under which language develops most easily and best, and about how teaching can support this development. And the implications of what we have yet to learn are even more profound.

I foresee a time when our school practice will be conceived as an expansion of children's language development, when we will be working in harmony with their natural language learning. Then we will see the importance of all language experience in school being useful and relevant to the learner. At that time, we will appreciate the strength of children as language learners and know how to support and build on such strength.

There will come a time in our schools when we will no longer talk about readiness as a separate set of prerequisites to learning but understand that what is learned must be functional in its own right, although it also forms a foundation for further learning.

I can see a time when the entire curriculum will be centered on integrated development of language and thinking. Teachers then will be aware of their essential double agenda. They will monitor children's language development in the context of their cognitive development, and they will understand that pupils need to keep their focus on the meaning they are expressing and comprehending, and not on language forms.

Literacy will soon come to be accepted as a natural development for all learners, and we will have school programs that involve whole language right from the beginning. The classroom will become a literate environment in which children read and write in increasingly more effective and varied ways.

This is no Utopian dream I've conjured up; I believe it is easily possible to achieve it. All it takes is hardworking, dedicated professionals who believe in kids and in themselves and who are willing to fight to make it happen. We've had some aspects before; there was a flourishing child study movement in the 1930s. But education, like all human endeavors, is not a totally rational institution. It takes constant efforts by all those concerned — particularly teachers and other school professionals — to keep the gains that have been made on improving practice and keep things moving forward through progressive application of new knowledge and theories.

The fight is a professional fight. In contemporary conditions, it is also a political fight. Researchers, scholars, and parents must join the school professionals in waging this fight on behalf of learners. Knowledge is of no use if it is not applied. And there is much new knowledge to apply to the teaching and learning of oral and written language.

Appendix

Angela M. Jaggar
Kathy T. Harwood

Suggested Reading List: Whole Language Theory, Practice, and Assessment

This bibliography is intended to acquaint readers with the sizable body of professional literature on language, literacy, and learning that has developed over the past twenty years. It was compiled in response to teachers' requests for information on how to design programs and implement instruction based on a sound theoretical base. It also reflects a specific orientation or philosophy. Taken as a whole, the selections in this bibliography provide a strong rationale and a solid knowledge base for holistic approaches to language teaching and learning.

The bibliography is divided into three major sections.

Theory: The Knowledge Base
Practice: Putting Theory to Use
Assessment: Observing the Language Learner

The entries in each section are subdivided by areas representing topics of major interest in the field. Each reference is listed only once, though many could have been listed in more than one section. The decision to place an item in a particular section or category was somewhat arbitrary but reflects our assessment of the focus emphasized or the use the reader can make of it. In addition, there is a section on Resources for Teachers, which includes a list of publishers from which indicated sources are available.

Though lengthy, this is not a comprehensive bibliography. It is a selective list of practical and theoretical sources that will be of interest to those concerned with language learning and teaching from birth through early childhood and the elementary school years. The entries were chosen on the basis of the soundness and accessibility of the content and the availability of the source. Readers will find the books and articles in this bibliography relatively easy reading or of moderate difficulty, requiring careful attention to the ideas but not contingent upon previous training in linguistics or other language related disciplines. Because of their importance or unique contribution to the field, other more technical references are included for further exploration. These are found mostly in the section on theory and research.

Theory: The Knowledge Base

Effective language teaching is based firmly on knowledge of children and how they grow and develop, and of language and how it is learned and used. New knowledge in a number of fields — developmental and cognitive psychology, education, linguistics, psycholinguistics, sociolinguistics, anthropology, and ethnography — has contributed greatly to our understanding of how children learn to speak, read, and write, and the important role context plays in the process. This work has led to dramatic changes in the way we view language and language learning, with far reaching implications for curriculum, instruction, and evaluation.

The readings in this section provide an overview of theory and research on ten issues that have received considerable attention in recent years:

1. the nature of language and literacy and the implications for schooling;
2. oral language development and use, including how children acquire linguistic and communicative competence in their native or a second language;
3. the relation of language to thought, that is, to intellectual development;
4. emergent and beginning literacy;
5. processes and stages in learning to spell;

6. the nature and development of reading;
7. the nature and development of writing;
8. relationships between reading and writing;
9. story development and response to literature; and
10. the nature of classroom discourse and its impact on learning.

Included are works dealing with the theory that underlies holistic, process oriented teaching. Those familiar with this work find it an exciting source of new knowledge and suggestions about how to create classroom contexts that promote language, literacy, and learning.

Nature of Language and Literacy: Implications for Schooling

Bloome, D. (Ed.). *Literacy and schooling.* Norwood, NJ: Ablex, 1987.

Bloome, D., and Knott, G. (Eds.). Building literacy. *Theory into Practice,* 1986, 25(2).

Burling, R. *English in black and white.* New York: Holt, Rinehart & Winston, 1975.

Christian, D., and Wolfram, W. *Exploring dialects.* Washington, DC: Center for Applied Linguistics, 1979.

Cook-Gumperz, J. (Ed.). *The social construction of literacy.* New York: Cambridge University Press, 1986.

Cummins, J. *Bilingualism and minority language children.* Toronto, Ontario: Ontario Institute for Studies in Education, 1981.

de Castell, S., Egan, K., and Luke, A. (Eds.). *Literacy, society, and schooling.* New York: Cambridge University Press, 1985.

Dulay, H., Burt, M., and Krashen, S. *Language two.* New York: Oxford University Press, 1982.

Fromkin, V., and Rodman, R. *An introduction to language,* fourth edition. New York: Holt, Rinehart & Winston, 1973.

Garb, P. *Word play: What happens when people talk.* New York: Bantam, 1975.

Halliday, M.A.K. *Explorations in the functions of language.* New York: Elsevier North-Holland, 1974.

Kroll, B.M., and Vann, R.J. *Exploring speaking-writing relationships: Connection and contrasts.* Urbana, IL: National Council of Teachers of English, 1981.

Langer, J.A. (Ed.). *Language, literacy, and culture: Issues of society and schooling.* Norwood, NJ: Ablex, 1987.

Olson, D.R., Torrance, N., and Hildyard, A. *Literacy, language, and learning.* New York: Cambridge University Press, 1985.

Penalosa, F. *Chicano sociolinguistics: A brief introduction.* Rowley, MA: Newbury House, 1980.

Smitherman, G. *Talking and testifying: The language of black America.* Boston: Houghton Mifflin, 1977.

Stubbs, M. *Language and literacy: The sociolinguistics of reading and writing.* London: Routledge & Kegan Paul, 1980.

Tannen, D. (Ed.). *Spoken and written language: Exploring orality and literacy.* Norwood, NJ: Ablex, 1982.

Taylor, D., and Dorsey-Gaines, C. *Growing up literate: Learning from innercity families.* Portsmouth, NH: Heinemann, 1988.

Trudgill, P. *Sociolinguistics: An introduction to language and society,* revised edition. Harmondsworth, England: Penguin Books, 1983.

Wallwork, J.F. *Language and people.* Portsmouth, NH: Heinemann, 1978.

Whiteman, M.F. (Ed.). *Variation in writing: Functional and linguistic cultural differences.* Hillsdale, NJ: Erlbaum, 1981.

Oral Language Acquisition, Use, and Development

Bloom, L., and Lahey, M. *Language development and language disorders.* New York: John Wiley & Sons, 1978.

Bruner, J. *Child's talk: Learning to use language.* New York: W.W. Norton, 1983.

Cazden, C.B. *Child language and education.* New York: Holt, Rinehart & Winston, 1972.

Dale, P.S. *Language development: Structure and function,* second edition. New York: Holt, Rinehart & Winston, 1976.

de Villiers, J.G., and Peter, A. *Language acquisition.* Cambridge, MA: Harvard University Press, 1978.

Ervin-Tripp, S., and Mitchell-Kernan, C. *Child discourse.* New York: Academic Press, 1977.

Franklin, M.B., and Barten, S.S. (Eds.). *Child language: A reader.* New York: Oxford University Press, 1988.

Galloway, C.M. (Ed.). Language use and acquisition. *Theory into Practice,* 1975, 4(5).

Garvey, C. *Children's talk.* Cambridge, MA: Harvard University Press, 1984.

Geller, L.G. *Wordplay and language learning for children.* Urbana, IL: National Council of Teachers of English, 1985.

Gleason, J.B. (Ed.). *The development of language.* Columbus, OH: Merrill, 1985.

Goodman, Y., and Goodman, K. Twenty questions about teaching language. *Educational Leadership,* 1981, 38(6), 437-442.

Halliday, M.A.K. *Learning how to mean: Explorations in the development of language.* New York: Elsevier North-Holland, 1975.

Heath, S.B. *Ways with words: Language, life, and work in communities and classrooms.* New York: Cambridge University Press, 1983.

Hopper, R., and Naremore, R.C. *Children's speech: A practical introduction to communications development.* New York: Harper & Row, 1973.

Krashen, S.D. *Principles and practice in second language acquisition.* Oxford, England: Pergamon Press, 1982.

Larsen-Freeman, D. *Discourse analysis in second language research.* Rowley, MA: Newbury House, 1980.

Lindfors, J.W. *Children's language and learning,* second edition. Englewood Cliffs, NJ: Prentice Hall, 1987.

Nelson, K. *Children's language.* New York: Gardner Press, 1978.

Ochs, E., and Schieffelin, B.B. *Developmental pragmatics.* New York: Academic Press, 1979.

Pinnell, G.S. (Ed.). *Discovering language with children.* Urbana, IL: National Council of Teachers of English, 1980.

Reich, P.A. *Language development.* Englewood Cliffs, NJ: Prentice Hall, 1986.

Rivers, W.M. *Communicating naturally in a second language: Theory and practice in language teaching.* New York: Cambridge University Press, 1986.

Sinclair, A., Jarsvella, R.J., and Levelt, W.J. (Eds.). *The child's conception of language.* New York: Springer-Verlag, 1978.

Smith, F. Demonstrations, engagement, and sensitivity: A revised approach to language learning. *Language Arts,* 1981, *58*(1), 103-112.

Tough, J. *The development of meaning: A study of children's use of language.* New York: John Wiley & Sons, 1977.

Wells, G. *Learning through interaction: The study of language development.* Cambridge, England: Cambridge University Press, 1981.

Wells, G., and Wells, J. Learning to talk and talking to learn. *Theory into Practice,* 1984, *23*(3), 190-197.

Wood, B.S. *Children and communication: Verbal and nonverbal language development.* Englewood Cliffs, NJ: Prentice Hall, 1976.

Thought and Language

Britton, J. *Language and learning.* Baltimore, MD: Penguin Books, 1970.

Bruner, J.S. *Actual minds, possible worlds.* Cambridge, MA: Harvard University Press, 1986.

Donaldson, M. *Children's minds.* New York: W.W. Norton, 1979.

Furth, H.G. *Piaget for teachers.* Englewood Cliffs, NJ: Prentice Hall, 1970.

Piaget, J. *The language and thought of the child.* New York: New American Library, 1974.

Vygotsky, L.S. *Mind in society: The development of higher psychological processes.* Translated and edited by M. Cole, V. John-Steiner, S. Scribner, and E. Souberman. Cambridge, MA: Harvard University Press, 1978.

Vygotsky, L.S. *Thought and language.* Translated by A. Kozulin. Cambridge, MA: MIT Press, 1986.

Yardley, A. *Young children thinking.* New York: Citation Press, 1973.

Emergent and Beginning Literacy: Writing and Reading

Bissex, G. GNYS AT WRK: *A child learns to write and read.* Cambridge, MA: Harvard University Press, 1980.

Bussis, A.M., Chittenden, E.A., Amarel, M., and Klausner, E. *Inquiry into meaning: An investigation of learning to read.* Hillsdale, NJ: Erlbaum, 1985.

Butler, D., and Clay, M. *Reading begins at home.* Portsmouth, NH: Heinemann, 1982.

Butler, D. *Cushla and her books.* Boston: The Horn Book, 1980.

Chomsky, C. Write first, read later. *Childhood Education,* 1971, *7*(6), 296-299.

Clark, M.M. *Young fluent readers: What can they teach us?* Portsmouth, NH: Heinemann, 1978.

Clay, M.M. Exploring with a pencil. *Theory into Practice,* 1977, *6*(5), 334-341.

Clay, M.M. *Observing young readers: Selected papers.* Portsmouth, NH: Heinemann, 1982.

Cochran-Smith, M. *The making of a reader.* Norwood, NJ: Ablex, 1984.

DeFord, D.E. Literacy: Reading, writing, and other essentials. *Language Arts,* 1981, *58*(6), 652-658.

Doake, D.B. *Reading begins at birth.* Richmond Hill, Ontario: Scholastic-TAB, 1988.

Downing, J. Children's developing concepts of spoken and written language. *Journal of Reading Behavior,* Winter 1971-1972, *4*, 1-19.

Dyson, A.H. Oral language: The rooting system for learning to write. *Language Arts,* 1981, *58*(7), 776-784.

Dyson, A.H. Reading, writing, and language: Young children solving the written language puzzle. *Language Arts,* 1982, *59*(8), 829-839.

Ehri, L., and Wilce, L. Does learning to spell help beginners learn to read words? *Reading Research Quarterly,* 1987, *22*(1) 47-65.

Farr, M. (Ed.). *Children's early writing development.* Norwood, NJ: Ablex, 1985.

Feitelson, D., Kita, B., and Goldstein, Z. Effects of listening to series stories on first graders' comprehension and use of language. *Research in the Teaching of English,* 1986, *20*(4), 339-356.

Ferreiro, E., and Teberosky, A. *Literacy before schooling.* Translated by K. Goodman Castro. Portsmouth, NH: Heinemann, 1982.

Goelman, H., Olberg, A., and Smith, F. *Awakening to literacy.* Portsmouth, NH: Heinemann, 1984.

Goodman, Y.M. The roots of literacy. M.P. Douglass (Ed.). *Reading: A humanizing experience.* Claremont, CA: Claremont Graduate School, 1980.

Hall, N. *The emergence of literacy.* Portsmouth, NH: Heinemann, 1987.

Harste, J.C., Woodward, V.A., and Burke, C.L. *Language stories and literacy lessons.* Portsmouth, NH: Heinemann, 1984.

Heath, S.B. What no bedtime story means: Narrative skills at home and school. *Language in Society,* 1982, *2*, 49-76.

Holdaway, D. *Stability and change in literacy learning.* Portsmouth, NH: Heinemann, 1984.

King, M.L., and Rentel, V. Toward a theory of early writing development. *Research in the Teaching of English,* 1979, *13*(3), 243-253.

Kontos, S. What preschool children know about reading and how they learn it. *Young Children,* November 1986, 58-86.

Lamme, L.L., and Childers, N.M. The composing processes of three young children. *Research in the Teaching of English,* 1983, *17*(1), 31-50.

Martinez, M., and Roser, N. Read it again: The value of repeated readings during storytime. *The Reading Teacher,* 1985, *38*(8), 782-786.

Mason, J.M. When do children begin to read: An exploration of four year old children's letter and word reading competencies. *Reading Research Quarterly,* 1980, *15*(2), 203-227.

Morrow, L.M. Young children's responses to one-to-one story readings in school settings. *Reading Research Quarterly,* 1988, *23*(1), 89-108.

Parker, R.P., and Davis, F.A. (Eds.). *Developing literacy: Young children's use of language*. Newark, DE: International Reading Association, 1983.

Resnick, L.B., and Weaver, P.A. (Eds.). *Theory and practice of early reading*, volume 1. Hillsdale, NJ: Erlbaum, 1979.

Roser, N.L. Relinking literature and literacy. *Language Arts*, 1987, *64*(1), 90-97.

Schickedanz, J.A. *More than the ABCs: The early stages of reading and writing*. Washington, DC: National Association for the Education of Young Children, 1986.

Snow, C. Literacy and language: Relationships during the preschool years. *Harvard Educational Review*, 1983, *52*(2), 165-189.

Sulzby, E. Children's emergent reading of favorite books: A developmental study. *Reading Research Quarterly*, 1985, *20*(4), 458-481.

Taylor, D. *Family literacy: Young children learning to read and write*. Portsmouth, NH: Heinemann, 1983.

Taylor, D., and Strickland, D.S. *Family storybook reading*. Portsmouth, NH: Heinemann, 1986.

Teale, W.H. Parents reading to their children: What we know and need to know. *Language Arts*, 1981, *58*(8), 902-910.

Teale, W.H. Toward a theory of how children learn to read and write naturally. *Language Arts*, 1982, *59*(6), 555-570.

Teale, W.H., and Sulzby, E. *Emergent literacy: Writing and reading*. Norwood, NJ: Ablex, 1986.

Torrey, J.W. Reading that comes naturally: The early reader. In T. Gary Waller and G.E. Mackinnon (Eds.), *Reading research: Advances in theory and practice*, volume 1. New York: Academic Press, 1979, 117-142.

Tovey, D.R., and Kerber, J.E. (Eds.). *Roles in literacy learning: A new perspective*. Newark, DE: International Reading Association, 1986.

White, D. *Books before five*. Portsmouth, NH: Heinemann, 1984.

Yaden, D.B., Jr., and Templeton, S. *Metalinguistic awareness and beginning literacy*. Portsmouth, NH: Heinemann, 1986.

Learning to Spell

Beers, J.W., and Beers, C.S. Vowel spelling strategies among first and second graders: A growing awareness of written words. *Language Arts*, 1980, *57*(2), 166-172.

Gentry, R.J. Learning to spell developmentally. *The Reading Teacher*, 1981, *34*(4), 378-381.

Henderson, E.H. *Learning to read and spell: The child's knowledge of words*. DeKalb, IL: Northern Illinois University Press, 1981.

Henderson, E.H., and Beers, J.W. (Eds.). *Developmental and cognitive aspects of learning to spell*. Newark, DE: International Reading Association, 1980.

Kamii, C., and Randazzo, M. Social interaction and invented spelling. *Language Arts*, 1985, *62*(2), 124-133.

Paul, R. Invented spelling in kindergarten. *Young Children*, 1976, *1*, 195-200.

Read, C. *Children's creative spelling*. London: Routledge & Kegan Paul, 1986.

Read, C. Preschool children's knowledge of English phonology. *Harvard Educational Review*, 1971, *1*(1), 1-34.

Wood, M. Invented spelling. *Language Arts*, 1982, *59*(7), 707-717.

Jaggar and Harwood

Reading: Process, Development, and Instruction

Allen, P.D., and Watson, D.J. (Eds.). *Findings of research in miscue analysis: Classroom implications.* Urbana, IL: National Council of Teachers of English, 1976.

Allington, R.L. Poor readers don't get to read much in reading groups. *Language Arts,* 1980, *57*(8), 872-876.

Anderson, B.V., and Barnitz, J.G. Cross cultural schemata and reading comprehension instruction. *Journal of Reading,* 1984, *28*(2), 102-108.

Anderson, R.C., Spiro, R.J., and Montague, W.E. *Schooling and the acquisition of knowledge.* Hillsdale, NJ: Erlbaum, 1977.

Berger, A., and Robinson, H.A. (Eds.). *Secondary school reading: What research reveals for classroom practice.* Urbana, IL: ERIC and the National Council of Teachers of English, 1982.

Bloome, D. Reading as a social process. *Language Arts,* 1985, *62*(2), 134-142.

Carey, R.F. (Ed.). *Findings of research in miscue analysis: Ten years later.* Urbana, IL: ERIC and the National Council of Teachers of English, 1987.

Clay, M.M. *Reading: The patterning of complex behavior,* second edition. Portsmouth, NH: Heinemann, 1979.

Durkin, D. What classroom observations reveal about reading comprehension instruction. *Reading Research Quarterly,* 1979, *14* (4) 481-533.

Durkin, D. What is the value of the new interest in reading comprehension? *Language Arts,* 1981, *58*(1), 23-43.

Flood, J. (Ed.). *Understanding reading comprehension.* Newark, DE: International Reading Association, 1984.

Galloway, C.M. (Ed.). Reading and language. *Theory into Practice,* 1977, *6*(5).

Gollasch, F.V. (Ed.). *Language and literacy: The selected writings of Kenneth S. Goodman,* volumes one and three. London: Routledge & Kegan Paul, 1982.

Goodman, K.S. The know-more and know-nothing movements in reading: A personal response. *Language Arts,* 1979, *56*(6), 657-663.

Goodman, K.S. (Ed.). *The psycholinguistic nature of the reading process,* second edition. Detroit, MI: Wayne State University Press, 1973.

Goodman, K.S., and Goodman, Y.M. Learning about psycholinguistic processes by analyzing oral reading. *Harvard Educational Review,* 1977, *7*(3), 317-333.

Goodman, K.S., Shannon, P., Freeman, Y.S., and Murphy, S. *Report card on basal readers.* New York: Richard C. Owen, 1988.

Harste, J.C., and Burke, C.L. A new hypothesis for reading research: Both the teaching and learning of reading are theoretically based. In P.D. Pearson (Ed.), *Reading: Theory, research, and practice.* Twenty-Sixth Yearbook of the National Reading Conference. Clemson, SC: National Reading Conference, 1977, 32-40.

Hedley, C.N., and Baratta, A.N. (Eds.). *Contexts of reading,* volume twenty-three. *Advances in discourse processes.* Norwood, NJ: Ablex, 1985.

King, D.F., and Watson, D.J. Reading as meaning construction. In B.A. Bushing and J.I. Schwartz (Eds.), *Integrating the language arts in the elementary school.* Urbana, IL: National Council of Teachers of English, 1983, 70-77.

Langer, J.A., and Smith-Burke, M.T. (Eds.). *Reader meets author/bridging the gap.* Newark, DE: International Reading Association, 1982.

Larrick, N. Illiteracy starts too soon. *Phi Delta Kappan,* November 1987, 184-189.

McConaughy, S.H. Developmental changes in story comprehension and levels of questioning. *Language Arts,* 1982, *59*(6), 580-589.

Meek, M. *Learning to read.* Portsmouth, NH: Heinemann, 1982.

Meek, M., Warlow, A., and Barton, G. (Eds.). *The cool web: The pattern of children's reading.* London: Bodley Head, 1977.

Ohnmacht, F.W. (Ed.). Reading in classrooms. *Journal of Reading Behavior,* 1982, *14*(4).

Orasanu, J. (Ed.). *Reading comprehension: From research to practice.* Hillsdale, NJ: Erlbaum, 1986.

Page, W.D. (Ed.). *Help for the reading teacher: New directions in research.* Urbana, IL: ERIC and the National Conference on Research in English, 1975.

Pearson, P.D. (Ed.). *Handbook of reading research.* New York: Longman, 1984.

Santa, C.M., and Hayes, B.L. *Children's prose comprehension: Research and practice.* Newark, DE: International Reading Association, 1981.

Shuy, R. (Ed.). *Linguistic theory: What can it say about reading?* Newark, DE: International Reading Association, 1977.

Singer, H., and Ruddell, R.B. (Eds.). *Theoretical models and processes of reading,* third edition. Newark, DE: International Reading Association, 1985.

Smith, F. *Comprehension and learning.* New York: Holt, Rinehart & Winston, 1973. (Available from Richard C. Owen.)

Smith, F. *Reading without nonsense.* New York: Teachers College Press, 1979.

Smith, F. *Understanding reading,* second edition. New York: Holt, Rinehart & Winston, 1978.

Spiro, R.J., Bruce, B.B., and Brewer, W.F. (Eds.). *Theoretical issues in reading comprehension.* Hillsdale, NJ: Erlbaum, 1980.

Stein, N.L., and Glenn, C.G. An analysis of story comprehension in elementary school children. In R.O. Freedle (Ed.), *New directions in discourse processing,* volume 2. Norwood, NJ: Ablex, 1979.

Weaver, C. *Reading process and practice: From sociopsycholinguistics to whole language.* Portsmouth, NH: Heinemann, 1988.

Writing: Process, Development, and Instruction

Applebee, A.N. *Contexts for learning to write: Studies of secondary school instruction.* Norwood, NJ: Ablex, 1984.

Bartlett, E.J. *Learning to write: Some cognitive and linguistic components.* Washington, DC: Center for Applied Linguistics, 1981.

Britton, J., Burgess, T., Martin, N., McLeod, A., and Rosen, H. *The development of writing abilities (11-18).* London: Macmillan Education, 1975. (Available from NCTE.)

Calkins, L.M. *Lessons from a child: On the teaching and learning of writing.* Portsmouth, NH: Heinemann, 1983.

Cooper, C.R., and Odell, L. *Research on composing: Points of departure.* Urbana, IL: National Council of Teachers of English, 1978.

Cowie, H. (Ed.). *The development of children's imaginative writing.* London: Croom Helm, 1984.

DeFord, D.E. (Ed.). Learning to write. *Theory into Practice,* 1980, *9*(3).

Edelsky, C. *Writing in a bilingual program.* Norwood, NJ: Ablex, 1986.

Flower, L., and Hayes, J.R. A cognitive process theory of writing. *College Composition and Communication,* 1981, *32*(4), 365-387.

Frederiksen, C.H., and Dominic, J.F. *Writing: Process, development, and communication.* Hillsdale, NJ: Erlbaum, 1981.

Freedman, S.W. (Ed.). *The acquisition of written language: Response and revision.* Norwood, NJ: Ablex, 1980.

Graves, D.H. An examination of the writing processes of seven year old children. *Research in the Teaching of English,* 1975, *9*(3), 227-241.

Graves, D.H. *Balance the basics: Let them write.* New York: Ford Foundation, 1978.

Graves, D.H. Research update: What children show us about revision. *Language Arts,* 1979, *6*(3), 312-319.

Kress, G. *Learning to write.* London: Routledge & Kegan Paul, 1982.

Kroll, B.M., and Wells, G. *Explorations in the development of writing: Theory, research, and practice.* New York: John Wiley & Sons, 1983.

Mayher, J.S., Lester, N., and Pradl, G. *Learning to write/learning to learn.* Montclair, NJ: Boynton/Cook, 1983.

Mosenthal, P., Tamore, L., and Walmsley, S.A. *Research on writing: Principles and methods.* New York: Longman, 1983.

Petrosky, A.R., and Bartholomae, D. (Eds.). *The teaching of writing.* Chicago: The University of Chicago Press, 1986.

Smith, F. *Writing and the writer.* New York: Holt, Rinehart & Winston, 1982.

Staton, J., Shuy, R.W., Peyton, J.K., and Reed, L. *Dialogue journal communication: Classroom linguistic, social, and cognitive views.* Norwood, NJ: Ablex, 1988.

Relationships between Reading and Writing

Birnbaum, J.C. The reading and composing behavior of selected fourth and seventh grade students. *Research in the Teaching of English,* 1982, *16*(3), 241-260.

Ferris, J., and Snyder, G. Writing as an influence on reading. *Journal of Reading,* 1986, *29*(9), 751-756.

Jensen, J.M. (Ed.). *Composing and comprehending.* Urbana, IL: National Conference on Research in English, 1984.

Kucer, S. The making of meaning: Reading and writing as parallel processes. *Written Communication,* 1985, *2*(3), 317-336.

Langer, J.A. *Children reading and writing: Structures and strategies.* Norwood, NJ: Ablex, 1986.

Petersen, B.T. (Ed.). *Convergences: Transactions in reading and writing.* Urbana, IL: National Council of Teachers of English, 1986.

Raphael, T.E. *The contexts of school based literacy.* New York: Random House, 1984.

Shanahan, T. The reading-writing relationship: Seven instructional principles. *The Reading Teacher,* 1988, *41*(7), 636-647.

Smith, F. Reading like a writer. *Language Arts,* 1983, *60*(5), 558-567.

Tierney, R.J., and LaZansky, J. The rights and responsibilities of readers and writers: A contractual agreement. *Language Arts,* 1980, *57*(6), 606-613.

Tierney, R.J., and Pearson, P.D. Toward a composing model of reading. *Language Arts*, 1983, *60*(5), 568-580.

Tierney, R.J., Anders, P., and Mitchell, J. *Understanding readers' understanding*. Hillsdale, NJ: Erlbaum, 1987.

Wilson, M.J. A review of recent research on the integration of reading and writing. *The Reading Teacher*, 1981, *34*(8), 896-901.

Story Development and Response to Literature

Applebee, A. *The child's concept of story*. Chicago: University of Chicago Press, 1978.

Beach R. Attitudes, social conventions, and response to literature. *Journal of Research and Development in Education*, 1983, *16*, 47-54.

Bettelheim, B. *The uses of enchantment: The meaning and importance of fairy tales*. New York: Knopf, 1977.

Britton, J. Viewpoints: The distinction between participant and spectator role language in research and practice. *Research in the Teaching of English*, 1984, *18*(3), 320-331.

Brown, G.H. Development of story in children's reading and writing. *Theory into Practice*, 1977, *5*(5), 357-362.

Bruce, B. Plans and discourse. *Text*, 1983, *3*, 253-259.

Cooper, C.R. (Ed.). *Researching response to literature and the teaching of literature: Points of departure*. Norwood, NJ: Ablex, 1985.

Dias, P.X. *Making sense of poetry: Patterns in the process*. Toronto, Ontario: Canadian Council of Teachers of English, 1987.

Favat, F.A. *Child and tale: The origins of interest*. Urbana, IL: National Council of Teachers of English, 1977.

Galda, L. Assuming the spectator stance: An examination of the responses of three young readers. *Research in the Teaching of English*, 1982, *16*(1), 1-20.

Galda, L. Readers, texts, and contexts: A response based view of literature in the classroom. *The New Advocate*, 1988, *1*(2), 92-102.

Golden, J., and Guthrie, J.T. Convergence and divergence in reader response to literature. *Reading Research Quarterly*, 1986, *21*(4), 408-422.

Hickman, J. Response to literature in a school environment. In Y.M. Goodman, M.M. Haussler, and D.S. Strickland (Eds.), *Oral and written language development research: Impact on the schools*. Urbana, IL: National Council of Teachers of English, 1982.

Huck, C.S., Hickman, J., and Zidonis, F. (Eds.). Children's literature. *Theory into Practice*, 1982, *21*(4).

Iser, W. *The act of reading: A theory of aesthetic response*. Baltimore, MD: Johns Hopkins University Press, 1978.

Petrosky, A. The inferences we make: Children and literature. *Language Arts*, 1980, *57*(2), 149-156.

Pradl, G.M. Learning how to begin and end a story. *Language Arts*, 1979, *56*(1), 21-25.

Purves, A.C., and Beach, R. *Literature and the reader: Research in response to literature, reading interests, and the teaching of literature*. Urbana, IL: National Council of Teachers of English, 1972.

Purves, A.C., and Rippere, V. *Elements of writing about a literary work: A study of response to literature.* Urbana, IL: National Council of Teachers of English, 1968.

Rosen, H. *Stories and meanings.* Sheffield, England: National Association for the Teaching of English, 1983. (Available from Heinemann.)

Rosenblatt, L.M. *Literature as exploration.* New York: Appleton-Century, 1938. (Available from NCTE.)

Rosenblatt, L.M. *The reader, the text, the poem.* Carbondale, IL: Southern Illinois University Press, 1978. (Available from NCTE.)

Rosenblatt, L.M. What facts does this poem teach? *Language Arts,* 1980, *57*(4), 386-394.

Schlager, N. Predicting children's choices in literature: A developmental approach. *Children's Literature in Education,* 1978, *9*(3), 136-142.

Terry, A. *Children's poetry preferences: A national survey of upper elementary grades.* Urbana, IL: National Council of Teachers of English, 1974.

Tucker, N. *The child and the book: A psychological and literary exploration.* New York: Cambridge University Press, 1981.

Classroom Discourse: Teacher-Student Talk and Its Impact on Learning

Barnes, D., and Todd, F. *Communication and learning in small groups.* London: Routledge & Kegan Paul, 1977.

Cazden, C.B. *Classroom discourse: The language of teaching and learning.* Portsmouth, NH: Heinemann, 1988.

Cazden, C.B., John, V.P., and Hymes, D. *Functions of language in the classroom.* New York: Teachers College Press, 1972.

Dillon, D., and Searle, D. The role of language in one first grade classroom. *Research in the Teaching of English,* 1981, *15*(4), 311-328.

Gilmore, P., and Glatthorn, A.A. *Children in and out of school: Ethnography and education.* Washington, DC: Center for Applied Linguistics, 1982.

Green, J.L. (Ed.). Communicating with young children. *Theory into Practice,* 1979, *8*(4).

Green, J., and Wallat, C. *Ethnography and language in educational settings.* Norwood, NJ: Ablex, 1980.

Heath, S.B. *Teacher talk: Language in the classroom.* Washington, DC: Center for Applied Linguistics, 1978.

McDermott, R.P. The ethnography of speaking and reading. In R.W. Shuy (Ed.), *Linguistic theory: What can it say about reading?* Newark, DE: International Reading Association, 1977.

Mehan, H. *Learning lessons: Social organization in the classroom.* Cambridge, MA: Harvard University Press, 1979.

Pinnell, G.S., and King, M.L. (Eds.). Access to meaning: Spoken and written language. *Theory into Practice,* 1984, *23*(5).

Rosen, C., and Rosen, J. *The language of primary school children.* London: Penguin Education for the Schools Council, 1973.

Spindler, G. *Doing the ethnography of schooling: Educational anthropology in action.* New York: Holt, Rinehart & Winston, 1982.

Torbe, M., and Protherough, R. (Eds.). *Classroom encounters: Language and English teaching.* London: Ward Lock Educational, 1976.

Tough, J. *Talk for teaching and learning.* London: Ward Lock Educational, 1979. (Available from Heinemann.)

Trueba, H.T., Guthrie, G.P., and Au, K.H. (Eds.). *Culture and the bilingual classroom: Studies in classroom ethnography.* Rowley, MA: Newbury House, 1981.

Wilkinson, L.C. *Communicating in the classroom.* New York: Academic Press, 1982.

Practice: Putting Theory to Use

Whole language is not a method of instruction but a theory or set of beliefs about language, literacy, and learning that guides teaching. Until recently, there were few books describing classroom applications of whole language theory. Fortunately, this is changing. The number of books published in the United States is growing rapidly, and many written in England, Canada, Australia, and New Zealand are now available through distributors in the United States, as indicated in the list that follows. Publications in this section were chosen because they will help teachers, administrators, and curriculum specialists put whole language theory to use in practice.

The list is divided into four categories. The publications in the first category focus primarily on teaching young children in nursery school, kindergarten, and primary grades. The learning experiences and language activities (shared reading, writing, drama, discussion, telling, and listening to stories) described in these sources are designed to stimulate the young child's natural curiosity, encourage the purposeful use of language, and foster positive attitudes toward language and learning. These references, and many in the next section, provide valuable suggestions about how to create learning environments and implement programs that are developmentally appropriate for children who are at the emergent and early stages of reading and writing.

The books and articles in the second category deal specifically with the teaching of reading or writing or both, and span the years from kindergarten through elementary and middle school. They describe and explain how to implement process oriented and integrated approaches to reading and writing and suggest materials,

Jaggar and Harwood

activities, and teaching strategies that are congruent with a holistic perspective. Of particular interest to many readers will be the materials that provide valuable information on making the change from a basal based reading program to one that is literature based.

Publications in the third category focus on language across the curriculum, discussing practice from a different point of view. These works are based on the premise that language and literacy development involves more than learning how to speak, how to read, and how to write; it also involves learning how to use language to communicate, think, and learn. They provide a strong rationale for integrating language arts and content area teaching and for using the four language processes – talking, writing, reading, and listening – as modes of learning in all areas of the curriculum. They also contain suggestions about how to design experiences in social studies, science, literature, math, and the arts that give students real problems to solve and tasks to do, individually and collaboratively, that will help them to think logically, read critically, talk, and write intelligently about the world they live in.

Items in the final category address the need for language policies to guide curriculum and instruction, material selection, staff development, and evaluation. These documents describe various strategies teachers, principals, and administrators can use to develop and implement school and districtwide policies based on a holistic view of language and learning across the curriculum.

Whole Language Approach to Teaching Young Children (N-3)

Altwerger, B., Edelsky, C., and Flores, B.M. Whole language: What's new? *The Reading Teacher,* 1987, *41*(2), 144-155.

Barrett, F.L. *A teacher's guide to shared reading.* Richmond Hill,Ontario: Scholastic-TAB, 1982.

Barton, B. *Tell me another.* Markham, Ontario: Pembroke, 1986. (Available from Heinemann.)

Baskwill, J., and Whitman, P. *A guide to classroom publishing.* Richmond Hill, Ontario: Scholastic-TAB, 1986.

Baskwill, J., and Whitman, P. *Whole language sourcebook.* Richmond Hill, Ontario: Scholastic-TAB, 1986.

Butler, A., and Turbill, J. *Towards a reading-writing classroom.* Rozelle, NSW, Australia: Primary English Teaching Association, 1984. (Available from Heinemann.)

Cullinan, B. E., and Carmichael, C.W. *Literature and young children*. Urbana, IL: National Council of Teachers of English, 1977.

Fields, M.V., and Lee, D. *Let's begin reading right*. Columbus, OH: Merrill, 1987.

Fox, M. *Teaching drama to young children*. Portsmouth, NH: Heinemann, 1986.

Goodman, K.S. *What's whole in whole language*. Portsmouth, NH: Heinemann, 1986.

Heald-Taylor, G. How to use predictable books for K-2 language arts instruction. *The Reading Teacher*, 1987, *40*(7), 656-661.

Heald-Taylor, G. *Whole language strategies for ESL students*. Buffalo, NY: OISE Press, 1986.

Heinig, R.B. *Creative drama resource books for kindergarten through grade 3*. Englewood Cliffs, NJ: Prentice Hall, 1987.

Holdaway, D. *The foundations of literacy*. Sydney, Australia: Ashton Scholastic, 1979. (Available from Heinemann.)

Jewell, M., and Zintz, M.V. *Learning to read naturally*. Dubuque, IA: Kendall/Hunt, 1986.

Lamme, L.L. (Ed.). *Learning to love literature: Preschool through grade 3*. Urbana, IL: National Council of Teachers of English, 1981.

Lynch, P. *Using big books and predictable books*. New York: Scholastic, 1986.

Massam, J., and Kulik, A. *And what else?* Auckland, New Zealand: Shortland Publications, 1986. (Available from Wright Group.)

McVitty, W. (Ed.). *Getting it together: Organising the reading-writing classroom*. Rozelle, NSW, Australia: Primary English Teaching Association, 1986. (Available from Heinemann.)

Peetoom, A. *Shared reading: Safe risks with whole books*. Richmond Hill, Ontario: Scholastic-TAB, 1986.

Reading in junior classes. Wellington, New Zealand: Department of Education, 1985. (Available from Richard C. Owen.)

Rhodes, L.K. I can read! Predictable books as resources for reading and writing instruction. *The Reading Teacher*, 1981, *34*(5), 511-518.

Salinger, T. *Language arts and literacy for young children*. Columbus, OH: Merrill, 1988.

Schwartz, J.I. *Encouraging early literacy: An integrated approach to reading and writing in N-3*. Portsmouth, NH: Heinemann, 1988.

Strickland, D.S., and Morrow, L.M. (Eds.). *Emerging literacy: Young children learn to read and write*. Newark, DE: International Reading Association, 1989.

Wilson, L. *Write me a sign: About language experience*. Nashville, TN: Thomas Nelson, 1979. (Available from Rigby.)

Teaching Reading and Writing from a Whole Language Perspective (K-8)

Allen, R.V., and Allen, C. *Language experience activities*. Boston: Houghton Mifflin, 1982.

Alvermann, D.E., Dillon, D.R., and O'Brien, D.G. *Using discussion to promote reading comprehension.* Newark, DE: International Reading Association, 1987.

Anderson, G.S. *A whole language approach to reading.* Lanham, MD: University Press of America, 1984.

Atwell, M.A., and Rhodes, L.K. Strategy lessons as alternatives to skills lessons in reading. *Journal of Reading,* 1984, *27*(8), 700-705.

Atwell, N. *In the middle: Writing, reading, and learning with adolescents.* Montclair, NJ: Boynton/Cook, 1987.

Bosma, B. *Fairy tales, fables, legends, and myths: Using folk literature in your classroom.* New York: Teachers College Press, 1987.

Burrows, A.T., Jackson, D.C., and Saunders, D.O. *They all want to write: Written English in the elementary school,* fourth edition. Hamden, CT: Library Professional Publications, 1984. (Available from IRA.)

Busching, B.A., and Schwartz, J.I. (Eds.). *Integrating the language arts in the elementary school.* Urbana, IL: National Council of Teachers of English, 1983.

Calkins, L.M. *The art of teaching writing.* Portsmouth, NH: Heinemann, 1986.

Cochrane, O., Cochrane, D., Scalena, S., and Buchman, E. *Reading, writing and caring.* Winnipeg, Canada: Whole Language Consultants, 1984. (Available from Richard C. Owen.)

Cullinan, B.E. (Ed.). *Children's literature in the reading program.* Newark, DE: International Reading Association, 1987.

D'Angelo, K. Correction behavior: Implications for reading instruction. *The Reading Teacher,* 1982, *35*(4), 395-398.

Devine, T.G. *Teaching reading comprehension: From theory to practice.* Boston: Allyn & Bacon, 1986.

Fehring, H., and Thomas, V. *The teaching of spelling.* Melbourne, Australia: Materials Production, Ministry of Education of Victoria, 1985. (Available from Rigby.)

Fitzgerald, J. Helping readers gain self-control over reading comprehension. *The Reading Teacher,* 1983, *37*(3), 249-253.

Five, C.L. From workbook to workshop: Increasing children's involvement in the reading process. *The New Advocate,* 1988, *1*(2), 103-113.

Fox, S.E., and Allen, V.G. *The language arts: An integrated approach.* New York: Holt, Rinehart & Winston, 1983.

Goodman, K.S., Smith, E.B., Meredith, R., and Goodman, Y.M. *Language and thinking in school: A whole language curriculum,* third edition. New York: Richard C. Owen Publishers, 1987.

Goodman, Y.M., and Burke, C. *Reading strategies: Focus on comprehension.* New York: Holt, Rinehart & Winston, 1980.

Goodman, Y.M., and Watson, D.J. A reading program to live with: Focus on comprehension. *Language Arts,* 1977, *54*(8), 868-879.

Gordon, N. (Ed.). *Classroom experience: The writing process in action.* Portsmouth, NH: Heinemann, 1984.

Graves, D.H. *Writing: Teachers and children at work.* Portsmouth, NH: Heinemann, 1983.

Graves, D.H., and Hansen, J. The author's chair. *Language Arts,* 1983, *60*(2), 176-183.

Hancock, J., and Hill, S. *Literature based reading programs at work.* Portsmouth, NH: Heinemann, 1987.

Hansen, J. *When writers read.* Portsmouth, NH: Heinemann, 1987.

Hansen, J., Newkirk, T., and Graves, D. *Breaking ground: Teachers relate reading and writing in the elementary school.* Portsmouth, NH: Heinemann, 1985.

Holdaway, D. *Independence in reading,* second edition. Gosford, NSW, Australia: Ashton Scholastic, 1980. (Available from Heinemann.)

Hornsby, D., Sukarna, D., and Parry, J. *Read on: A conference approach to reading.* Sydney, Australia: Martin Educational, 1986. (Available from Rigby.)

Hudson, C., and O'Toole, M. *Spelling: A teacher's guide.* Drouin, Australia: Landmark, 1983. (Available from Rigby.)

Johnson, T.D., and Louis, D.R. *Literacy through literature.* Richmond Hill, Ontario: Scholastic-TAB, 1987.

Kimmel, M.M., and Segel, E. *For reading out loud! A guide to sharing books with children.* New York: Delacorte, 1983.

Klein, M.L. *Teaching reading comprehension and vocabulary: A guide for teachers.* Englewood Cliffs, NJ: Prentice Hall, 1988.

Koskinen, P.S., Gambrell, L.B., Kapinus, B.A., and Heathington, B.S. Retelling: A strategy for enhancing students' reading comprehension. *The Reading Teacher,* 1988, *41*(9), 892-897.

Lee, D.M., and Rubin, J.B. *Children and language: Reading and writing, talking and listening.* Belmont, CA: Wadsworth, 1979.

Livo, N.J., and Rietz, S.A. *Storytelling activities.* Littleton, CO: Libraries Unlimited, 1987.

Loughlin, C.E., and Martin, M.D. *Supporting literacy: Developing effective learning environments.* New York: Teachers College Press, 1987.

McConaughy, S.H. Using story structure in the classroom. *Language Arts,* 1980, *57*(2), 157-165.

McCracken, R.A. Initiating sustained silent reading. *Journal of Reading,* 1971, *14*(8), 521-524, 582-583.

McCracken, R.A., and McCracken, M. Modeling is the key to sustained silent reading. *The Reading Teacher,* 1978, *31*(4), 406-408.

McCracken, R.A., and McCracken, M. *Stories, songs, and poetry for teaching reading and writing.* New York: Teachers College Press, 1986.

Moffett, J., and Wagner, B.J. *Student centered language arts and reading, K-13: A handbook for teachers.* Boston: Houghton Mifflin, 1983.

Morrow, L.M. Retelling stories: A strategy for improving young children's comprehension, concept of story structure, and oral language complexity. *Elementary School Journal,* 1985, *39*(6), 564-570.

Newman, J.M. (Ed.). *Whole language: Theory in use.* Portsmouth, NH: Heinemann, 1985.

Ogle, D. K-W-L: A teaching model that develops active reading of expository text. *The Reading Teacher,* 1986, *39*(6), 564-570.

Parry, J., and Hornsby, D. *Write on: A conference approach to writing.* Sydney, Australia: Martin Educational, 1985. (Available from Rigby.)

Pearson, P.D., and Johnson, D.D. *Teaching reading comprehension.* New York: Holt, Rinehart & Winston, 1978.

Purves, A.C., and Monson, D.L. *Experiencing children's literature.* Glenview, IL: Scott, Foresman, 1984.

Reardon, S.J. The development of critical readers: A look into the classroom. *The New Advocate,* 1988, *1*(1), 52-60.

Rhodes, L.K., and Dudley-Marling, C. *Readers and writers with a difference.* Portsmouth, NH: Heinemann, 1988.

Scardamalia, M., Bereiter, C., and Fillion, B. *Writing for results: A sourcebook of consequential composing activities.* Toronto, Ontario: The Ontario Institute for Studies in Education, 1981.

Schwartz, S. *All write: A teacher's guide to writing, grades K to 6.* Toronto, Ontario: The Ontario Institute for Studies in Education, 1987.

Sloan, P., and Latham, R. *Teaching reading is....* Nashville, TN: Thomas Nelson, 1981. (Available from Rigby.)

Stauffer, R. *The language experience approach to the teaching of reading,* second edition. New York: Harper & Row, 1980.

Strickland, D.S. Building children's knowledge of stories. In J. Osborn, P.T. Wilson, and R.C. Anderson (Eds.), *Reading education: Foundation for a literate America.* Lexington, MA: D.C. Heath, 1985.

Tierney, R.J., Readence, J.E., and Dishner, E.K. *Reading strategies and practices: Guide for improving instruction.* Boston: Allyn & Bacon, 1980.

Trelease, J. *The read-aloud handbook.* New York: Penguin, 1982. (Available from IRA.)

Turbill, J. *No better way to teach writing.* Rozelle, NSW, Australia: Primary English Teaching Association, 1982. (Available from Heinemann.)

Turbill, J. *Now, we want to write.* Rozelle, NSW, Australia: Primary English Teaching Association, 1983. (Available from Heinemann.)

Walshe, R.D. *Every child can write.* Rozelle, NSW, Australia: Primary English Teaching Association, 1982. (Available from Rigby.)

Watson, D., and Crowley, P. How can we implement a whole language approach? In C. Weaver (Ed.), *Reading process and practice.* Portsmouth, NH: Heinemann, 1988.

Watson, D.J. (Ed.). *Ideas with insights: Language arts for the elementary school.* Urbana, IL: National Council of Teachers of English, 1988.

Language across the Curriculum: Definition, Rationale, and Implementation

Barnes, D. *From communication to curriculum.* Harmondsworth, England: Penguin, 1976.

Barnes, D., Britton, J., and Rosen, H. *Language, the learner, and the school.* Harmondsworth, England: Penguin, 1969.

Barr, M., D'Arcy, P., and Healy, M.K. *What's going on? Language/learning episodes in British and American classrooms, grades 4-13.* Montclair, NJ: Boynton/Cook, 1982.

Britton, J. *Prospect and retrospect: Selected essays of James Britton.* G.M. Pradl (Ed.). Montclair, NJ: Boynton/Cook, 1982.

Bullock, Alan. *A language for life.* London: Her Majesty's Stationery Office, 1975.

Christenbury, L., and Kelly, P. *Questioning: A path to critical thinking.* Urbana, IL: National Council of Teachers of English, 1983.

Dalton, J. *Adventures in thinking: Creative thinking and cooperative talk in small groups.* Nashville, TN: Thomas Nelson, 1986. (Available from Rigby.)

● Dillon, D. (Ed.). Drama as a learning medium. *Language Arts,* 1988, *65*(1).

● Dillon, D. (Ed.). Language across the curriculum. *Language Arts,* 1983, *60*(6).

Dillon, D. (Ed.). Literary discourse as a way of knowing. *Language Arts,* 1988, *65*(3).

Dillon, D. (Ed.). Transactional discourse. *Language Arts,* 1986, *63*(2).

Emig, J. Writing as a mode of learning. In D. Goswami and M. Butler (Eds.), *The web of meaning.* Montclair, NJ: Boynton/Cook, 1983.

Fillion, B. Let me see you learn. *Language Arts,* 1983, *60*(6), 702-710.

Fillion, B. Reading as inquiry: An approach to literature learning. *English Journal,* 1981, *70,* 39-45.

Fulwiler, T. *The journal book.* Portsmouth, NH: Heinemann, 1987.

● Fulwiler, T., and Young, A. (Eds.). *Language connections: Writing and reading across the curriculum.* Urbana, IL: National Council of Teachers of English, 1982.

Gamberg, R., Kwak, W., Hutchings, M., and Altheim, J. *Learning and loving it: Theme studies in the classroom.* Portsmouth, NH: Heinemann, 1988.

Gerbrandt, G.L. *An idea book for acting out and writing language, K-8.* Urbana, IL: National Council of Teachers of English, 1974.

Heimlich, J.E., and Pittelman, S.D. *Semantic mapping: Classroom applications.* Newark, DE: International Reading Association, 1986.

● Hennings, D.G. *Teaching communication and reading skills in the content area.* Bloomington, IN: Phi Delta Kappa, 1982.

● Jenkinson, E.B. (Ed.). Writing across the curriculum. *Phi Delta Kappan,* 1988, *69*(10).

Jones, A., and Mulford, J. (Eds.). *Children using language: An approach to English in the primary school.* London: Oxford University Press, 1971.

Klein, M.L. Designing a talk environment for the classroom. *Language Arts,* 1979, *56*(6), 647-656.

Klein, M.L. *Talk in the language arts classroom.* Urbana, IL: ERIC and National Council of Teachers of English, 1977.

Macrorie, K. *Searching writing.* Montclair, NJ: Boynton/Cook, 1980.

Marland, M. *Language across the curriculum.* Portsmouth, NH: Heinemann, 1977.

Martin, N. *Mostly about writing.* Montclair, NJ: Boynton/Cook, 1983.

Martin, N., D'Arcy, P., Newton, B., and Parker, R. *Writing and learning across the curriculum 11-16.* London: Ward Lock Educational, 1980.(Available from Heinemann-Boynton/Cook.)

McCaslin, N. *Children and drama,* second edition. New York: Longman, 1981.

Medway, P. *Finding a language: Autonomy and learning in school.* London: Writers and Readers Publishing Cooperative, 1980.

Medway, P., and Torbe, M. *The climate for learning.* Montclair, NJ: Boynton/Cook, 1981.

Jaggar and Harwood

Moffett, J. *Teaching the universe of discourse.* Boston: Houghton Mifflin, 1983.

Moore, D.W., Readence, J.E., and Rickelman, R.J. *Prereading activities for content area reading and learning,* second edition. Newark, DE: International Reading Association, 1989.

Norton, D.E. Using a webbing process to develop children's literature units. *Language Arts,* 1982, *59*(4), 348-356.

Robinson, H.A. *Teaching reading, writing, and study strategies: The content areas,* third edition. Boston: Allyn & Bacon, 1983.

Smardo, F.A. Using children's literature to clarify science concepts in early childhood programs. *The Reading Teacher,* 1982, *36*(3), 267-273.

Stewart-Dore, N. *Writing and reading to learn.* Rozelle, NSW, Australia: Primary English Teaching Association, 1986. (Available from LINK.)

Tchudi, S.N., and Huerta, M.C. *Teaching writing in the content areas: Middle school/junior high.* Urbana, IL: National Education Association of the United States, 1983. (Available from NCTE.)

Tchudi, S.N., and Tchudi, S.J. *Teaching writing in the content areas: Elementary school.* Washington, DC: National Education Association, 1983.

Thaiss, C. *Language across the curriculum in the elementary grades.* Urbana, IL: ERIC and the National Council of Teachers of English, 1986.

Virginia Department of Education. *Plain talk about learning and writing across the curriculum,* Commonwealth of Virginia, 1987.

Wilson, M. How can we teach reading in the content areas? In C. Weaver (Ed.), *Reading process and practice.* Portsmouth, NH: Heinemann, 1988.

Establishing School Language Policies

Bates, J. Educational policies that support language development. *Theory into Practice,* 1984, *23*(3), 255-260.

Fillion, B. Language across the curriculum: Examining the place of language in our schools. In T. Newkirk (Ed.), *To compose: Teaching writing in the high school.* Portsmouth, NH: Heinemann, 1986.

Martin, N. Initiating and implementing a policy. In M. Marland (Ed.), *Language across the curriculum.* Portsmouth, NH: Heinemann, 1977.

National Association for the Teaching of English (England). *Language across the curriculum: Guidelines for schools.* London: Ward Lock Educational, 1976.

Ontario Ministry of Education. *Language across the curriculum: A resource document for principals and teachers.* Toronto, Ontario: Ontario Ministry of Education, 1978.

Rosen, H. Towards a language policy across the curriculum. In D. Barnes, J. Britton, and H. Rosen (Eds.), *Language, the learner, and the school,* revised edition. London: Penguin, 1971.

Somerfield, M., Torbe, M., and Ward, C. *A framework for reading: Creating a policy in the elementary school.* North American adaptation by Arlene M. Pillar. Portsmouth, NH: Heinemann, 1985.

Toronto Board of Education. *A guideline for a school language policy.* Toronto, Ontario: Language Study Centre, 1983.

Assessment: Observing the Language Learner

Recent advances in the field have raised serious questions about the validity and usefulness of traditional methods of evaluation, particularly testing. As a result, educators and researchers are exploring other methods and procedures, ones more congruent with holistic teaching goals and practice. They are finding that informed observation is the most effective way to evaluate children's language and learning. By listening carefully to what children say and watching what they do when they talk, read, and write, we can learn about their knowledge and concepts of oral and written language, their strategies for processing language, their stages of development, and their uses of language. Ongoing, systematic observation, i.e., kid watching, yields the most useful kinds of data to assess student progress, diagnose problems, determine program effectiveness, and plan instruction that is responsive to students' needs.

The references in this kid watching section: (1) address issues in language assessment and provide a rationale for using naturalistic observation and performance samples as alternatives to testing; (2) discuss how observation can become an integral part of teaching and evaluation; (3) examine different aspects of spoken and written language (e.g., form and function, structure and meaning, process and product) and suggest conceptual frameworks for what to look for and how to interpret what we see and hear; and (4) describe, either directly or indirectly by their treatment of language, specific techniques and procedures that can be used to observe, document, and assess what children know and can do with language as they read, write, talk, and learn across the curriculum.

General Sources

Almy, M., and Genishi, C. *Ways of studying children,* revised edition. New York: Teachers College Press, 1979.

Baskwill, J., and Whitman, P. *Evaluation: Whole language, whole child.* New York: Scholastic, 1988.

Black, J.K. Those "mistakes" tell us a lot. *Language Arts,* 1980, *57*(5), 508-513.

Fagan, W.T., Cooper, C.R., and Jensen, J.M. *Measures for research and evaluation in the English language arts.* Urbana, IL: ERIC and the National Council of Teachers of English, 1975.

Fagan, W.T., Jensen, J.M., and Cooper, C.R. *Measures for research and evaluation in the English language arts,* volume two. Urbana, IL: ERIC and the National Council of Teachers of English, 1985.

Froese, V. Language assessment: What we do and what we should do! *Canadian Journal of English Language Arts,* 1988, *11*(1), 33-40.

Genishi, C., and Dyson, A.H. *Language assessment in the early years.* Norwood, NJ: Ablex, 1984.

Goodman, K.S., Goodman, Y.M., and Hood, W.J. *The whole language evaluation book.* Portsmouth, NH: Heinemann, 1989.

Goodman, Y.M. Kid watching: An alternative to testing. *National Elementary Principals Journal,* 1988, *7*(4), 41-45.

Jaggar, A., and Smith-Burke, M.T. (Eds.). *Observing the language learner.* Newark, DE: International Reading Association, 1985.

Marek, A., Howard, D., Disinger, J., Jacobson, D., Earle, N., Goodman, Y., Hood, W., Woodley, C., Woodley, J., Wortman, J., and Wortman, R. *A kid watching guide: Evaluation for whole language classrooms.* Occasional Papers, Program in Language and Literacy. Tucson, AZ: University of Arizona, 1984.

McKenzie, M., and W. Kernig. Evaluation learning. *The Urban Review,* 1976, *9*(1), 59-72.

Stibbs, A. *Assessing children's language: Guidelines for teachers.* London: Ward Lock Educational, 1979. (Available from NCTE.)

Watson, D.J. Valuing and evaluating the learners and their language. In D.J. Watson (Ed.), *Ideas and insights: Language arts in the elementary school.* Urbana, IL: National Council of Teachers of English, 1987, 209-219.

Wilkinson, A., Barnsely, G., Hanna, P., and Swan, M. *Assessing language development.* New York: Oxford University Press, 1980.

Oral Language Assessment

Black, J.K. Formal and informal means of assessing the communicative competence of kindergarten children. *Research in the Teaching of English,* 1979, *3*(1), 49-68.

Black, J.K. There's more to language than meets the ear: Implications for evaluation. *Language Arts,* 1979, *56*(5), 526-532.

Chukovsky, K. *From two to five.* Translated and edited by M. Morton. Berkeley, CA: University of California Press, 1963.

Clay, M.M., Gill, M., Glynn, T., McNaughton, T., and Salmon, K. *Record of oral language and biks and gutches.* Portsmouth, NH: Heinemann, 1983.

Dalton, J. Guidelines for evaluation. In *Adventures in thinking: Creative thinking and cooperative talk in small groups.* Nashville, TN: Thomas Nelson, 1986, 181-187. (Available from Rigby.)

de Villiers, Peter A., and Jill, G. *Early language.* Cambridge, MA: Harvard University Press, 1979.

Dillon, D. Assessing language and learning. In M. Maguire and A. Pare (Eds.), *Patterns of development.* Ottawa, Canada: Canadian Council of Teachers of English, 1985, 97-113. (Available from NCTE.)

Gilmore, P. Research currents: Assessing sub-rosa skills in children's language. *Language Arts,* 1984, *61*(4), 384-391.

Gonzales, P.C., and Hansen-Krening, N. Assessing the language learning environment in classrooms. *Educational Leadership,* 1981, *38*(6), 450-453.

Gorman, T. Language assessment and language teaching: Innovation and interaction. In G. Wells and J. Nicholls (Eds.), *Language and learning: An interactional perspective*. Philadelphia: Falmer Press, 1985, 125-133.

Kolczynski, R.G. Ways of looking at language use. In Gay Su Pinnell (Ed.), *Discovering language with children*. Urbana, IL: National Council of Teachers of English, 1980, 113-118.

Lazarus, P.G. What children know and teach about language competence. *Theory into Practice*, 1984, *23*(3), 225-238.

Lund, N.J., and Duchan, J.F. *Assessing children's language in naturalistic contexts*, second edition. Englewood Cliffs, NJ: Prentice Hall, 1988.

Martin, N., Williams, P., Wilding, J., Hemmings, S., and Medway, P. *Understanding children talking*. London: Penguin Books, 1976.

Michaels, S. Listening and responding: Hearing the logic in children's classroom narratives. *Theory into Practice*, 1984, *23*(3), 218-224.

Paley, V.G. Wally's stories. Cambridge, MA: Harvard University Press, 1981.

Pinnell, G.S. Language in primary classrooms. *Theory into Practice*, 1975, *4*(5), 318-327.

Shafer, R.E., Claire, S., and Smith, K. *Language functions and school success*. Glenview, IL: Scott, Foresman, 1983.

Steinberg, Z.D., and Cazden, C.B. Children as teachers—of peers and ourselves. *Theory into Practice*, 1979, *18*(4), 258-266.

Tough, J. *Listening to children talking*. London: Ward Lock Educational, 1976. (Available from Heinemann.)

Tough, J. *Talking and learning*. London: Ward Lock Educational, 1977. (Available from Heinemann.)

Wallat, C., and Green, J.L. Social rules and communicative contexts in kindergarten. *Theory into Practice*, 1979, *18*(4), 275-284.

Weeks, T. *Born to talk*. Rowley, MA: Newbury House, 1979.

Wells, G. *The meaning makers: Children learning language and using language to learn*. Portsmouth, NH: Heinemann, 1986.

Wilkinson, A., Stratta, L., and Dudley, P. *The quality of listening*. London: Macmillan, 1974.

Wilkinson, L.C. Research currents: Peer group talk in elementary school. *Language Arts*, 1984, *61*(2), 164-169.

Williams, F., Hopper, R., and Natalicio, D.S. *The sounds of children*. Englewood Cliffs, NJ: Prentice Hall, 1977.

Early Literacy Assessment: Emergent and Beginning Reading and Writing

Bagban, M. *Our daughter learns to read and write*. Newark, DE: International Reading Association, 1984.

Blackburn, E. Common ground: Developing relationships between reading and writing. *Language Arts*, 1984, *61*(4), 367-375.

Cambourne, B., and Turbill, J. *Coping with chaos*. Rozelle, NSW, Australia: Primary Teaching English Association, 1987. (Available from Heinemann.)

Clay, M.M. *A diagnostic survey and concepts of print test, sand, and stones*. Portsmouth, NH: Heinemann, 1979.

Clay, M.M. *The early detection of reading difficulties,* third edition. Portsmouth, NH: Heinemann, 1985.

Clay, M.M. *What did I write?* Portsmouth, NH: Heinemann, 1979.

Clay, M.M. *Writing begins at home.* Portsmouth, NH: Heinemann, 1987.

Cohn, M. Observations of learning to read and write naturally. *Language Arts,* 1981, *58*(5), 549-556.

Doake, D.B. Reading like behavior: Its role in learning to read. In A. Jaggar and M.T. Smith-Burke (Eds.), *Observing the language learner.* Newark, DE: International Reading Association, 1985.

Eeds, M. Holistic assessment of coding ability. In S.M. Glazer, L.W. Searfoss, and L.M. Gentile (Eds.), *Reexamining reading diagnosis: New trends and procedures.* Newark, DE: International Reading Association, 1988, 48-67.

Giacobbe, M.E. Kids can write the first week of school. *Learning,* 1981, *9*, 130-132.

Goodman, Y.M., and Altwerger, B. Print awareness in preschool children: A study of the development of literacy in preschool children. Occasional Papers, Arizona Center for Research and Development. Tucson, AZ: University of Arizona, 1981.

Heald-Taylor, B.G. Predictable literature selections and activities for language arts instruction. *The Reading Teacher,* 1987, *41*(1), 6-12.

Heald-Taylor, B.G. Scribble in first grade writing. *The Reading Teacher,* 1984, *38*(1), 4-8.

Holdaway, D. Literacy learning before school. *Foundations of literacy.* Sydney, Australia: Ashton Scholastic, 1979, 38-63. (Available from Heinemann.)

Klein, A., and Schickedanz, J. Preschoolers write messages and receive their favorite books. *Language Arts,* 1980, *57*(7), 742-749.

Lamme, L.L. *Growing up writing.* Washington, DC: Acropolis Books, 1984.

McDonell, G.M., and Osburn, E.B. Beginning writing: Watching it develop. *Language Arts,* 1980, *57*(3), 310-314.

McDonell, G.M., and Osburn, E.B. New thoughts about reading readiness. *Language Arts,* 1978, *55*(1), 26-29.

McKenzie, M. The beginnings of literacy. *Theory into Practice,* 1977, *6*(5), 315-324.

Meek, M., Fox, C., Dombey, H., Whitehead, M., Walter, C., and Stierer, B. *Opening moves: Work in progress in the study of children's language development.* London: Institute of Education, London University, 1983. (Available from Heinemann.)

Milz, V.E. First graders can write: Focus on communication. *Theory into Practice,* 1980, *19*(3), 179-185.

Morris, D. Concept of word: A developmental phenomenon in the beginning reading and writing processes. *Language Arts,* 1981, *58*(6), 659-667.

Newman, J. *The craft of children's writing.* New York: Scholastic, 1984.

Resnick, M., Roth, J., Aaron, P., Scott, J., Wolking, W., Larsen, J., and Packer, A. Mothers reading to infants: A new observational tool. *The Reading Teacher,* 1987, *40*(9), 888-895.

Teale, W.H., Heibert, E.H., and Chittenden, E.A. Assessing young children's literacy development. *The Reading Teacher,* 1987, *40*(8), 772-777.

Temple, C., Nathan, R., Burris, B., and Temple, F. *The beginnings of writing,* second edition. Boston: Allyn & Bacon, 1988.

Templeton, S. Young children invent words: Developing concepts of wordness. *The Reading Teacher,* 1980, *33*(4), 454-459.

Weiss, M.M., and Hagen, R. A key to literacy: Kindergartner's awareness of the functions of print. *The Reading Teacher,* 1988, *41*(6), 574-578.

Yaden, D. Understanding stories through repeated read alouds: How many does it take? *The Reading Teacher,* 1988, *41*(6), 556-561.

Reading Assessment

Anderson, G.S. Evaluation of reading. In *A whole language approach to reading.* Lanham, MD: University Press of America, 1984, 89-182.

Applebee, A. A sense of story. *Theory into Practice,* 1977, *6*(5), 342-347.

Bailey, J., Brazee, P., Chiavaroli, S., Herbeck, J., Lechner, T., Lewis, D., McKittrick, A., Redwine, L., Reid, K., Robinson, B., and Spear, H. Problem solving our way to alternative evaluation procedures. *Language Arts,* 1988, *65*(4), 364-373.

Bartolli, J., and Botel, M. Toward a more congruent and ecological evaluation. In *Reading/learning disability: An ecological approach.* New York: Teachers College Press, 1988, 187-216.

Cullinan, B.E., Harwood, K.T., and Galda, L. The reader and the story: Comprehension and response. *Journal of Research and Development in Education,* 1983, *16*(3), 29-39.

Galda, L. Research in response to literature. *Journal of Research and Development in Education,* 1983, *16*(1), 1-7.

Glazer, S.M., Searfoss, L.W., and Gentile, L.M. (Eds.). *Reexamining reading diagnosis: New trends and procedures.* Newark, DE: International Reading Association, 1988.

Golden, J. Children's concept of story in reading and writing. *The Reading Teacher,* 1984, *37*(7), 578-581.

Goodman, Y.M. Retellings of literature and the comprehension process. *Theory into Practice,* 1982, *21*(4), 301-307.

Goodman, Y.M., Watson, D.J., and Burke, C.L. *Reading miscue inventory: Alternative procedures.* New York: Richard C. Owen, 1987.

Griffin, P. How and when does reading occur in the classroom? *Theory into Practice,* 1977, *16*(5), 376-383.

Hickman, J. A new perspective on response to literature: Research in an elementary school setting. *Research in the Teaching of English,* 1981, *15*(4), 343-354.

Hickman, J. Children's response to literature: What happens in the classroom. *Language Arts,* 1980, *7*(5), 524-529.

Hornsby, D., Sukarna, D., and Parry, P. Record keeping and evaluation. In *Read on: A conference approach to reading.* Sydney, Australia: Martin Educational, 1986, 129-143. (Available from Rigby.)

Johnston, P., and Pearson, P.D. Assessment: Responses to exposition. In A. Berger and H.A. Robinson (Eds.), *Secondary school reading.* Urbana, IL: ERIC and National Conference on Research in English, 1982.

King, M. Evaluating reading. *Theory into Practice,* 1977, *6*(5), 407-418.

Mikkelsen, N. Patterns of story development in children's response to literature. In M. Maguire and A. Pare (Eds.), *Patterns of development.* Ottawa, Canada: The Canadian Council of Teachers of English, 1985. (Available from NCTE.)

Pikulski, J.J., and Shanahan, T. (Eds.). *Approaches to the informal evaluation of reading.* Newark, DE: International Reading Association, 1982.

Rubin, S., and Gardner, H. Once upon a time: The development of sensitivity to story structure. In C.R. Cooper (Ed.), *Researching response to literature and the teaching of literature: Points of departure.* Norwood, NJ: Ablex, 1985, 169-189.

Squire, J.R. (Ed.). The state of reading assessment. *The Reading Teacher,* 1987, *40*(8).

Weaver, C. How can we assess readers' strengths and begin to determine their instructional needs? In C. Weaver (Ed.), *Reading process and practice: From sociopsycholinguistics to whole language.* Portsmouth, NH: Heinemann, 1988, 321-363.

Writing Assessment

Blackburn, E. Stories never end. In J. Hansen, T. Newkirk, and D. Graves (Eds.), *Breaking ground: Teachers relate reading and writing in the elementary school.* Portsmouth, NH: Heinemann, 1985.

Blatt, G., and Rosen, L.M. Writing: A window on children and their reading. *English Quarterly,* 1987, *20*(2), 121-130.

Burgess, C., Burgess, T., Cartland, L., Chambers, R., Hedgeland, J., Levine, N., Mole, J., Newsome, B., Smith, H., and Torbe, M. *Understanding children writing.* London: Penguin, 1973.

Calkins, L.M. When children want to punctuate: Basic skills belong in context. *Language Arts,* 1980, *57*(5), 567-573.

Cooper, C.R., and Odell, L. *Evaluating writing: Describing, measuring, judging.* Urbana, IL: National Council of Teachers of English, 1977.

Edelsky, C., and Smith, K. Is that writing—or are those marks just a figment of your curriculum? *Language Arts,* 1984, *61*(1), 24-32.

Estabrook, I.W. Talking about writing—developing independent writers. *Language Arts, 59*(7), 696-706.

Florio, S., and Clark, C. The functions of writing in an elementary classroom. *Research in the Teaching of English,* 1982, *16*(2), 115-129.

Forester, A.D. Learning to spell by spelling. *Theory into Practice,* 1980, *19*(3), 186-193.

Gentry, R. An analysis of developmental spelling in GNYS AT WRK. *The Reading Teacher,* 1982, *36*(2), 192-201.

Gentry, R. *Spel...is a four letter word.* New York: Scholastic, 1987.

Hannan, E., and Hamilton, G. Writing: What to look for, what to do. *Language Arts,* 1984, *61*(4), 364-367.

Harris, J., and Wilkinson, J. *Reading children's writing: A linguistic view.* London: Allen & Unwin, 1986.

Hourd, M.L., and Cooper, G.E. *Coming into their own.* Portsmouth, NH: Heinemann, 1971.

Jacobs, S.E. Investigative writing: Practice and principles. *Language Arts,* 1984, *61*(4), 356-364.

Jaggar, A.M., Carrara, D., and Weiss, S.E. Research currents: The influence of reading on children's narrative writing (and vice versa). *Language Arts,* 1986, *63*(3), 292-300.

Kreeft, J. Dialogue writing: Bridge from talk to essay writing. *Language Arts,* 1984, *61*(2), 141-150.

Kroll, B.M., and Anson, M.C. Analysing structure in children's fictional narratives. In H. Cowie (Ed.), *The development of children's imaginative writing.* London: Croom Helm, 1984, 153-184.

Myers, M. *A procedure for writing assessment and holistic scoring.* Urbana, IL: National Council of Teachers of English, 1980.

Newkirk, T., and Atwell, N. (Eds.). *Understanding writing: Ways of observing, learning, and teaching K-8,* second edition. Portsmouth, NH: Heinemann, 1988.

Perera, K. *Children's writing and reading: Analysing classroom language.* Oxford, England: Basil Blackwell, 1984.

Pollock, L.A. An exploratory analysis of children's diaries. In H. Cowie (Ed.), *The development of children's imaginative writing.* London: Croom Helm, 1984, 89-108.

Samway, K. Formal evaluation of children's writing: An incomplete story. *Language Arts,* 1987, *64*(3), 289-298.

Searle, D., and Dillon, D. Responding to student writing: What is said or how it is said. *Language Arts,* 1980, *7*(7), 773-781.

Searle, D., and Stevenson, M. An alternative assessment program in language arts. *Language Arts,* 1987, *64*(3) 278-284.

Weaver, C. Welcoming errors as signs of growth. *Language Arts,* 1982, *59*(5), 438-444.

Zutell, J. Some psycholinguistic perspectives on children's spelling. *Language Arts,* 1978, *55*(7), 844-850.

Resources for Teachers

Whole Language Newsletters

Dialogue. Center for Applied Linguistics, 1118 22 Street NW, Washington, DC 10037.

Teachers networking: The whole language newsletter. Richard C. Owen Publishers, Rockefeller Center, PO Box 819, New York, NY 10185.

The web. Ohio State University, Room 20, Ramseyer Hall, 29 W. Woodruff, Columbus, OH 43210.

Whole language newsletter. Scholastic-TAB Publications, 123 Newkirk Road, Richmond Hill, Ontario, Canada L4C 3G5.

Sources of Children's Literature

Cullinan, B.E. *Literature and the child,* second edition. New York: Harcourt Brace Jovanovich, 1989.

Haviland, V. (Ed.). *Children and literature: Views and reviews.* Glenview, IL: Scott, Foresman, 1973.

Hearne, B. *Choosing books for children: A commonsense guide.* New York: Delacorte, 1981.

Hearne, B., and Kaye, M. *Celebrating children's books.* New York: Lothrop, 1986.

Hopkins, L.B. *Pass the poetry please!* New York: Citation Press, 1972.

Huck, C.S. *Children's literature in the elementary school,* third edition. New York: Holt, Rinehart & Winston, 1976.

Larrick, N. *A parent's guide to children's reading.* New York: Bantam, 1982.

Monson, D.L. (Ed.). *Adventuring with books.* Urbana, IL: National Council of Teachers of English, 1985.

Sims, R. *Shadow and substance: Afro-American experience in contemporary children's fiction.* Urbana, IL: National Council of Teachers of English, 1982.

Sutherland, Z., and Arbuthnot, M.H. *Children and books,* seventh edition. Glenview, IL: Scott, Foresman, 1986.

Tway, E. *Reading ladders for human relations.* Washington, DC: American Council on Education, 1981.

Vandergrift, K.E. (Ed.). *Child and story: The literary connection.* New York: Neal-Schuman, 1981.

White, M.L. (Ed.). *Children's literature: Criticism and response.* Columbus, OH: Merrill, 1976.

List of Publishers' Addresses

Heinemann Educational Books & Boynton/Cook, 70 Court Street, Portsmouth, NH 03801.

International Reading Association, 800 Barksdale Road, PO Box 8139, Newark, DE 19714.

National Council of Teachers of English, 1111 Kenyon Road, Urbana, IL 61801.

Richard C. Owen Publishers, PO Box 819, New York, NY 10185.

Rigby Education, 454 S. Virginia Street, Crystal Lake, IL 60014.

Scholastic, 2931 E. McCarty Street, PO Box 7502, Jefferson City, MO 65102.

Scholastic-TAB Publications, 123 Newkirk Road, Richmond Hill, Ontario, Canada L4C 3G5.

The Wright Group, 10949 Technology Place, San Diego, CA 92127.

References Cited in This Book

Allen, P.D., and Watson, D.J. (Eds.). *Findings of research in miscue analysis: Classroom applications*. Urbana, IL: National Council of Teachers of English, 1976.

Allington, R.L. If they don't read much, how they ever gonna get good? *Journal of Reading*, 1977, *21*, 57-61.

Allington, R.L. Poor readers don't get to read much in reading groups. *Language Arts*, 1980, *57*, 872-876.

Amarel, M. *The teacher as observer*. Occasional paper. Harrisburg, PA: Department of Education, Right to Read Office, 1980.

Anderson, L.M., Evertson, C.M., and Brophy, J.E. An experimental study of effective training in first grade groups. *Elementary School Journal*, 1979, *79*, 193-223.

Anderson, R.C., Hiebert, E.H., Scott, J.A., and Wilkinson, I.A.G. *Becoming a nation of readers: The report of the Commission on Reading*. Washington, DC: The National Institute of Education, 1985.

Applebee, A.N. Children's construal of stories and related genres as measured with repertory grid techniques. *Research in the Teaching of English*, 1976, *10* (3), 226-238.

Barnes, D. *From communication to curriculum*. London: Penguin Books, 1976.

Barnes, D. Language strategies in learning. In M. Torbe and R. Protherough (Eds.), *Classroom encounters: Language and English education*. London: Ward Lock Educational, 1978.

Baron, J. Orthographic and word specific mechanisms in children's reading of words. *Child Development*, 1979, *50*, 50-72.

Barr, M., D'Arcy, P., and Healey, M.K. *What's going on? Language learning episodes in British and American classrooms, grades 4-13*. Montclair, NJ: Boynton/Cook, 1982.

Benton, M. Children's response to stories. *Children's literature in education*, 1979, *10* (2), 68-85.

Berman, P., and McLaughlin, M.W. *Federal programs supporting educational change. The findings in review*, volume 4. Santa Monica, CA: Rand Corporation, 1975.

Bissex, G. GYNS AT WRK: *A child learns to write and read*. Cambridge, MA: Harvard University Press, 1980.

Bloom, D., and Green, J. Directions in the sociolinguistic study of reading. In P.D. Pearson (Ed.), *Handbook of reading research*. New York: Longman, 1984, 395-421.

Bloom, L. *Language development: Form and function in emerging grammars*. Cambridge, MA: MIT Press, 1970.

Bloom, L., and Lahey, M. *Language development and language disorders*. New York: Wiley, 1978.

Board, P. *Toward a theory of instructional influence: Aspects of the instructional environment and their influence on children's acquisition of reading*. Unpublished doctoral dissertation, University of Toronto, 1982.

Bowerman, M. Words and sentences: Uniformity, individual variation, and shifts over time in patterns of acquisition. In F.D. Minifi and L.L. Lloyd (Eds.), *Communicative and cognitive abilities: Early behavioral assessment*. Baltimore, MD: University Park Press, 1978, 349-396.

Britton, J. English: Retrospect and prospect. In G. Pradl (Ed.), *Prospect and retrospect: Selected essays of James Britton*. Montclair, NJ: Boynton/Cook, 1982.

Brown, A.L. Development, schooling, and the acquisition of knowledge about knowledge: Comments on chapter 7 by Nelson. In R.C. Anderson, R.J. Spiro, and W.E. Montague (Eds.), *Schooling and the acquisition of knowledge*. Hillsdale, NJ: Erlbaum, 1977.

Brown, A.L. Knowing when, where, and how to remember: A problem of metacognition. In R. Glaser (Ed.), *Advances in instructional psychology*. Hillsdale, NJ: Erlbaum, 1978.

Brown, D.L., and Biggs, L.D. Young children's concepts of print. In M.R. Sampson (Ed.), *The pursuit of literacy: Early reading and writing*. Dubuque, IA: Kendall/Hunt, 1986, 49-55.

Brown, G. Development of story in children's reading and writing. *Theory into Practice*,

1977, *16* (5), 357-362.

Brown, R. *A first language*. Cambridge, MA: Harvard University Press, 1973.

Brown, R. Introduction to *Talking to children: Language input and acquisition*. C. Snow and C. Ferguson (Eds.). Cambridge, England: Cambridge University Press, 1977, 1-27.

Bullowa, M. (Ed.). *Before speech: The beginning of interpersonal communication*. Cambridge, England: Cambridge University Press, 1979.

Bussis, A.M., Chittenden, E.A., Amarel, M., and Klausner, E. *Inquiry into meaning: An investigation of learning to read*. Hillsdale, NJ: Erlbaum, 1985.

Carrasco, R.L., Vera, A., and Cazden, C.B. Aspects of bilingual students' communicative competence in the classroom: A case study. In R. Duran (Ed.), *Latino language and communicative behavior*. Discourse processes: Advances in research and theory, volume 4. Norwood, NJ: Ablex, 1981.

Cazden, C.B. Adult assistance to language development: Scaffolds, models, and direct instruction. In R. Parker and F. Davis (Eds.), *Developing literacy: Young children's use of language*. Newark, DE: International Reading Association, 1983.

Cazden, C.B. *Child language and education*. New York: Holt, Rinehart and Winston, 1972.

Cazden, C.B. Toward a social educational psychology—with Soviet help. *Contemporary Educational Psychology*, 1980, *5*, 196-201.

Cazden, C.B., Cox, M., Dickinson, D., Steinberg, Z., Stone, C. "You all gonna hafta listen": Peer teaching in a primary classroom. In W.A. Collins (Ed.), *Children's language and communication*. Hillsdale, NJ: Erlbaum, 1979, 183-231.

Chomsky, C.S. When you still can't read in third grade: After decoding, what? In S.J. Samuels (Ed.), *What research has to say about reading instruction*. Newark, DE: International Reading Association, 1978.

Clark, H.H., and Chase, W.G. On the process of comparing sentences against pictures. *Cognitive Psychology*, 1972, *3*, 472-517.

Clark, H.H., and Clark, E.V. *Psychology and language*. New York: Harcourt Brace Jovanovich, 1977.

Clay, M.M. *The early detection of reading difficulties*, second and third editions. Auckland, New Zealand: Heinemann, 1979, 1985.

Clay, M.M. Exploring with a pencil. *Theory into Practice*, 1977, *16* (5), 334-341.

Clay, M.M. Implementing reading recovery: Systemic adaptations to an educational innovation. *New Zealand Journal of Educational Studies*, 1987, *22*, 351-358.

Clay, M.M. *Observing young readers*. Auckland, New Zealand: Heinemann, 1982.

Clay, M.M. *Reading: The patterning of complex behavior*. Auckland, New Zealand: Heinemann, 1979.

Clay, M.M. *What did I write?* Auckland, New Zealand: Heinemann, 1975.

Clay, M.M., and Oates, R. *Round about twelve*. Auckland, New Zealand: Department of Education, University of Auckland, 1984.

Clay, M.M., and Watson, B. An inservice program for reading recovery teachers. In M.M. Clay (Ed.), *Observing young readers*. Portsmouth, NH: Heinemann, 1982, 192-200.

Cochran-Smith, M. *The making of a reader*. Norwood, NJ: Ablex, 1984.

Cohen, D. The effect of literature on vocabulary and reading achievement. *Elementary English*, 1958, *45*, 209-213, 217.

Cohen, D., and Stern, V. *Observing and recording the behavior of young children*, second edition. New York: Teachers College Press, 1979.

Cullinan, B.E., Jaggar, A., and Strickland, D. Language expansion for black children in the primary grades: A research report. *Young Children*, 1974, *29*, 98-112.

DeFord, D.D., Pinnell, G.S., Lyons, C.A., and Young, P. *Follow-up studies of the reading recovery program*. Technical Report. Columbus, OH: Ohio State University, 1987.

DeStefano, J. *Language, the learner, and the school*. New York: John Wiley & Sons, 1978.

DeVilliers, J.G., and DeVilliers, P.A. Competence and performance in child languages: Are children really competent to judge? *Journal of Child Language*, 1974, *1*, 11-22.

DeVilliers, J.G., and DeVilliers, P.A. Semantics and syntax in the first two years: The output

171

of form and function and the form and function of the input. In F.D. Minifi and L.L. Lloyd (Eds.), *Communicative and cognitive abilities: Early behavioral assessment.* Baltimore, MD: University Park Press, 1978, 309-348.

Dewey, J. *How we think: A restatement of the relation of reflective thinking to the educative process.* Boston: D.C. Heath, 1933.

Dillon, D., and Searle, D. The role of language in one first grade classroom. *Research in the Teaching of English*, 1981, *15*, 311-328.

Doake, D. *Book experience and emergent reading in preschool children.* Doctoral dissertation, University of Alberta, 1981.

Doehring, D.G., and Aulls, N.W. The interactive nature of reading acquisition. *Journal of Reading Behavior*, 1979, *11*, 27-40.

Donaldson, M. *Children's minds.* New York: Norton, 1978.

Dreeben, R., and Barr, R. Educational policy and the working of schools. In L.S. Schulman and G. Sykes (Eds.), *Handbook of teaching and policy.* New York: Longman, 1983.

Durkin, D. What does research say about the time to begin reading instruction? *Journal of Educational Research*, 1970, *64*, 521-556.

Dybdahl, C. Languaging about language. In M. Haussler, D. Strickland, and Y. Goodman (Eds.), *Oral and written language development research: Impact on the schools.* Urbana, IL: National Council of Teachers of English, 1980.

Edelsky, C., Draper, R., and Smith, K. Hookin' em in at the start of school in a "whole language" classroom. *Anthropology and Education Quarterly*, 1983, *14* (4), 257-281.

Edwards, A.D., and Furlong, V.J. *The language of teaching.* London: Heinemann, 1978.

Ehri, L.C., and Wilce, L.S. The mnemonic value of orthography among beginning readers. *Journal of Educational Psychology*, 1979, *71*, 26-40.

Favat, F. *Child and tale: The origins of interest.* Urbana, IL: National Council of Teachers of English, 1977.

Ferreiro, E., and Teberosky, A. *Literacy before schooling.* London: Heinemann, 1979.

Flavell, J.H. *Cognitive development.* Englewood Cliffs, NJ: Prentice Hall, 1977.

Fletcher, P., and Garman, M. (Eds.). *Language acquisition: Studies in first language development.* Cambridge, England: Cambridge University Press, 1979.

Francis, H. Children's experience of reading and notions of units in language. *British Journal of Educational Psychology*, 1973, *43*, 17-23.

Frederiksen, C.H. Inference in preschool children's conversations: A cognitive perspective. In J. Green and C. Wallat (Eds.), *Ethnography and language in educational settings.* Norwood, NJ: Ablex, 1981.

Gambrell, L.B. Reading in the primary grades: How often, how long? In M.R. Sampson (Ed.), *The pursuit of literacy: Early reading and writing.* Dubuque, IA: Kendall/Hunt, 1986, 102-108.

Gelman, R. Cognitive development. *Annual Review of Psychology*, 1978, *29*, 297-332.

Gelman, R. Logical capacity of very young children: Number invariance rules. *Child Development*, 1972, *43*, 75-90.

Gesell, A. *The first five years of life.* New York: Harper, 1940.

Ghiselin, B. *The creative process.* New York: Mentor Books, 1955.

Gleitman, L.R., Gleitman, H., and Shipley, E.F. The emergence of child as grammarian. *Cognition*, 1972, *1*, 137-163.

Glickman, C.D. The supervisor's challenge: Changing the teacher's work environment. *Educational Leadership*, 1985, *42*, 38-45.

Goelman, H., Olberg, A., and Smith, F. (Eds.). *Awakening to literacy.* Portsmouth, NH: Heinemann, 1984.

Goldstein, D.M. Cognitive linguistic functioning and learning to read in preschoolers. *Journal of Educational Psychology*, 1976, *68*, 680-688.

Goodenough, W. *Culture, language, and society.* Reading, MA: Addison-Wesley, 1971.

Goodlad, J., and Klein, M.F. *Behind the classroom door.* Worthington, OH: Charles A. Jones, 1970.

Goodman, K.S. Behind the eye: What happens in reading. In K.S. Goodman and O.S. Niles (Eds.), *Reading: Process and program*. Urbana, IL: National Council of Teachers of English, 1970.

Goodman, K.S. Reading: A psycholinguistic guessing game. In H. Singer and R. Ruddell (Eds.), *Theoretical models and processes of reading*, second edition. Newark, DE: International Reading Association, 1975, 259-272.

Goodman, K.S. *What's whole in whole language?* Portsmouth, NH: Heinemann, 1986.

Goodman, K.S., Meredith, R., and Smith, E.B. *Language and thinking*, second edition. New York: Richard Owen Publishing, 1986.

Goodman, Y.M. Children coming to know literacy. In W.H. Teale and E. Sulzby (Eds.), *Emergent literacy: Writing and reading*. Norwood, NJ: Ablex, 1986, 1-4.

Goodman, Y.M. The development of initial literacy. In H. Goelman, A. Olberg, and F. Smith (Eds.), *Awakening to literacy*. Portsmouth, NH: Heinemann, 1984.

Goodman, Y.M. Roots of literacy. In Malcolm Douglass (Ed.), *Reading: A humanizing experience*. Claremont, CA: Claremont Graduate School, 1980.

Graves, D. An examination of the writing processes of seven year old children. *Research in the Teaching of English*, 1975, *9*, 227-241.

Graves, D. *Writing: Teachers and children at work*. Portsmouth, NH: Heinemann, 1983.

Green, J.L., Harker, J., and Golden, J. Lesson construction: Differing views. In G. Noblit and W. Pink (Eds.), *Schooling in social context: Qualitative studies*. Norwood, NJ: Ablex, 1987.

Greenlaw, J., and Jaggar, A.M. *The relations among teachers' concepts about reading, their beliefs about reading instruction, and selected program characteristics*. Final Report. Denton, TX: North Texas University, in press.

Halliday, M.A.K. *Language as social semiotic*. Baltimore, MD: University Park Press, 1978.

Halliday, M.A.K. *Learning how to mean*. London: Arnold, 1975.

Halliday, M.A.K. Relevant models of language. *Educational Review*, 1969, *22*, 26-37.

Harste, J., and Burke, C. Examining instructional assumptions: The child as informant. *Theory into Practice*, 1980, *19* (3), 170-178.

Harste, J., Burke, C., and Woodward, V. *Language stories and literacy lessons*. Portsmouth, NH: Heinemann, 1984.

Haussler, M. *Transitions into literacy: A psycholinguistic analysis of beginning reading in kindergarten and first grade children*. Doctoral dissertation, University of Arizona, 1982.

Heap, J. What counts as reading? Limits to certainty in assessment. *Curriculum Inquiry*, 1980, *10*, 265-292.

Heath, S.B. Ethnography: Defining the essentials. In P. Gilmore and A. Glatthorn (Eds.), *Children in and out of school*. Washington, DC: Center for Applied Linguistics, 1982.

Heath, S.B. *Ways with words: Language, life, and work in communities and classrooms*. Cambridge, England: Cambridge University Press, 1983.

Hegelson, S., Blosser, P., and Howe, R. *The status of precollege science, mathematics, and social studies in U.S. high schools: An overview and summary of three studies*, volume 1. Washington, DC: Government Printing Office, 1978.

Hickman, J. A new perspective in response to literature in an elementary school environment. *Research in the Teaching of English*, 1981, *15* (14), 343-354.

Hodgkinson, H.L. *All one system: Demographics of education, kindergarten through graduate school*. Washington, DC: Institute for Educational Leadership, 1985.

Hodgkinson, H.L. The right schools for the right kids. *Educational Leadership*, 1988, *45*, 10-14.

Holdaway, D. *The foundations of literacy*. Sydney, Australia: Ashton Scholastic, 1979.

Holdaway, D. The structure of natural learning as a basis for literacy instruction. In M.R. Sampson (Ed.), *The pursuit of literacy: Early reading and writing*. Dubuque, IA: Kendall/Hunt, 1986, 56-72.

Holland, K. *The impact of reading recovery programs on parents and home literacy contexts*.

Unpublished doctoral dissertation, Ohio State University, 1987.

Howe, R. The prospect for children in the United States. *Phi Delta Kappan*, 1986, *68* (4), 191-196.

Huck, C.S., and Pinnell, G.S. *The reading recovery project in Columbus, Ohio: Pilot year, 1984-1985*. Technical Report. Columbus, OH: Ohio State University, 1985.

Ingram, D. If and when transformations are acquired by children. In D.P. Dato (Ed.), *GURT 1975. Developmental psycholinguistics: Theory and applications*. Washington, DC: Georgetown University Press, 1977, 99-127.

Jackson, N.E. *Passing the individual differences test: A cram course for developmental psychologists*. Seattle, WA: University of Washington, Child Development Research Group, 1971. (ED 174358)

Jaggar, A.M. On observing the language learner: Introduction and overview. In A.M. Jaggar and M.T. Smith-Burke (Eds.), *Observing the language learner*. Newark, DE: International Reading Association and the National Council of Teachers of English, 1985.

Johnston, P.H. Assessment in reading. In P.D. Pearson (Ed.), *Handbook of reading research*. New York: Longman, 1984, 147-182.

Kamler, B. One child, one teacher, one classroom: The story of one piece of writing. *Language Arts*, 1980, *57*, 680-693.

Kendall, J.R., and Hood, J. Investigating the relationship between comprehension and word recognition: Oral reading analysis of children with comprehension or word recognition disabilities. *Journal of Reading Behavior*, 1979, *11*, 41-48.

King, D., and Holbrook, C. *TAWL groups: Teachers supporting teachers*. Presented at an IRA/NCTE workshop, "Making Language and Literacy Programs More Effective," Denver, Colorado, 1983.

Kinsbourne, M., and Hiscock, M. Does cerebral dominance develop? In S.J. Segalowitz and F.A. Gruber (Eds.), *Language development and neurological theory*. New York: Academic Press, 1977.

Klima, E.S., and Bellugi-Klima, U. Syntactic regularities in the speech of children. In J. Lyons and R. Wales (Eds.), *Psycholinguistics papers*. Edinburgh, Scotland: Edinburgh University Press, 1966, 183-208.

LaBerge, D., and Samuels, S.J. Toward a theory of automatic information processing in reading. *Cognitive Psychology*, 1974, *6*, 293-323.

Lasley, T.J., and Galloway, C.M. Achieving professional status: A problem in what teachers believe. *The Clearing House*, 1983, *56*, 5-8.

Lavine, C. Differentiation of letter-like forms in prereading children. *Developmental Psychology*, 1977, *13* (2), 89-94.

Lawrence, G., and Branch, J. Peer support system as the heart of inservice education. *Theory into Practice*, 1978, *17*, 245-247.

Lawrence, G. *Patterns of effective inservice education*. Tallahassee, FL: Florida Department of Education, 1974. (ED 176424)

Leiberman, Ann. *Teachers, their world, and their work*. Alexandria, VA: Association for Supervision and Curriculum Development, 1984.

Leong, C.K. Laterality and reading proficiency in children. *Reading Research Quarterly*, 1980, *15*, 185-202.

Lewis, M. *Origins of intelligence*. New York: Plenum, 1976.

Lindfors, J. *Children's language and learning*. Englewood Cliffs, NJ: Prentice Hall, 1980.

Lock, Andrew (Ed.). *Action, gesture, and symbol: The emergence of language*. New York: Academic Press, 1978.

Lord, C. Variations in the pattern of acquisition of negation. *Papers and reports on child language development*. Palo Alto, CA: Committee in Linguistics, Stanford University, 1974, 78-86.

Lyons, C.A., Pinnell, G.S., Young, P., and DeFord, D. *Report of the Ohio reading recovery project: Year 1, implementation.* Technical Report. Columbus, OH: Ohio State University, 1987.

Maratsos, M., Kuczaj, S.A., Fox, D.E.C., and Chalkley, M.A. Some empirical studies in the acquisition of transformational relations: Passives, negatives, and the past tense. In W.A. Collins (Ed.), *Children's language and communication.* Hillsdale, NJ: Erlbaum, 1979, 1-43.

Mason, J.M. Early reading from a developmental perspective. In P.D. Pearson (Ed.), *Handbook of reading research.* New York: Longman, 1984, 505-544.

Mathews, N.N., Hunt, E.B., and MacLeod, C.M. Strategy choice and strategy training in sentence-picture verification. *Journal of Verbal Learning and Verbal Behavior,* 1980, *19,* 531-548.

McCormick, C.E., and Mason, J.M. Fostering reading for Head Start children with little books. In J.B. Allen and J. Mason (Eds.), *Reducing the risks for children in reading.* Portsmouth, NH: Heinemann, 1988.

McCutcheon, G. Curriculum theory, curriculum practice: A gap or the Grand Canyon. In Alex Molnar (Ed.), *Current thought on curriculum.* Alexandria, VA: Association for Supervision and Curriculum Development, 1985.

Meek, M. *Achieving literacy: Longitudinal studies of adolescents learning to read.* London: Routledge & Kegan Paul, 1983.

Mehan, H. *Learning lessons.* Cambridge, MA: Harvard University Press, 1979.

Moffett, J., and Wagner, B.J. *Student-centered language arts and reading: A handbook for teachers,* second edition. Boston: Houghton Mifflin, 1976.

Moore, T.E., and Harris, A.E. Language and thought in Piagetian theory. In L.S. Siegel and F.J. Brainerd (Eds.), *Alternatives to Piaget: Critical essay on the theory.* New York: Academic Press, 1977, 131-152.

Neisser, U. *Cognitive psychology.* New York: Appleton-Century-Crofts, 1976.

Nelson, K. Structure and strategy in learning to talk. *Monographs of the Society for Research in Child Development,* 1973, *38,* 149.

Newman, J.M. (Ed.). *Whole language: Theory and use.* Portsmouth, NH: Heinemann, 1985.

Nisbet, J., and Broadfoot, P. *The impact of research on policy and practice in education.* Aberdeen, Scotland: Aberdeen University Press, 1980.

Oller, J.W., Jr., and Perkins, K. *Language in education: Testing the tests.* Rowley, MA: Newbury House, 1978.

Papandropoulou, I., and Sinclair, H. What is a word? *Human Development,* 1974, *17,* 241-258.

Perrone, V. Supporting teacher growth. *Childhood Education,* 1978, 298-302.

Peters, A. Language learning strategies: Does the whole equal the sum of the parts? *Language,* 1977, *53,* 560-573.

Piaget, J. *The Language and thought of the child.* New York: Meridian Books, 1969.

Pinnell, G.S. Creating literacy communities to help children at risk of failure. In J.B. Allen and J. Mason (Eds.), *Reducing the risks for children in reading.* Portsmouth, NH: Heinemann, in press.

Pinnell, G.S. Helping teachers help children at risk: Insights from the reading recovery program. *Peabody Journal of Education,* 1985, *62,* 70-85.

Pinnell, G.S. Helping teachers see how readers read: Staff development through observation. *Theory into Practice,* 1987, *26,* 1.

Pinnell, G.S., Lyons, C.A., DeFord, D., and Young, P. *The reading recovery project in Columbus, Ohio: 1986-1987.* Technical Report. Columbus, OH: Ohio State University, 1987.

Pinnell, G.S., Short, K., Lyons, C.A., and Young, P. *The reading recovery project in Columbus, Ohio: 1985-1986.* Technical Report. Columbus, OH: Ohio State University, 1986.

Platt, N.G. *The context for writing: A descriptive study of one family-grouped, informal first* and *second grade classroom.* Unpublished doctoral dissertation, Ohio State University, 1982.

Posner, G.J. *Field experience: A guide to reflective teaching.* New York: Longman, 1985.

Pratt, C., and Grieve, R. Language awareness in children. *Education Research and Perspectives,* 1980, *7* (University of Western Australia).

Ramer, A. Syntactic styles in emerging language. *Journal of Child Language,* 1976, *3,* 49-62.

Raven, R. Language acquisition in a second language environment. In J.W. Oller, Jr. and J.C. Richards (Eds.), *Focus on the learner.* Rowley, MA: Newbury House, 1973, 136-144.

Read, C. *Children's categorization of speech sound in English.* NCTE Committee on Research Report No. 17. Urbana, IL: National Council of Teachers of English, 1975a.

Read, C. Lessons to be learned from the preschool orthographers. In E.H. Lenneberg (Ed.), *Foundations of language development: A multidisciplinary approach,* volume 2. New York: Academic Press, 1975b.

Roedell, W., Jackson, N.E., and Robinson, H.B. *Gifted young children.* New York: Columbia Teachers College Press, 1980.

Sarason, S. *The creation and setting of future societies.* San Francisco, CA: Jossey-Bass, 1972.

Saylor, J.G. *Who planned the curriculum?* West Lafayette, IN: Kappa Delta Phi, 1982.

Schwartz, J.I. Metalinguistic awareness: A study of verbal play in young children. Urbana, IL: National Council of Teachers of English and ERIC Clearinghouse on Reading, 1977.

Scribner, S., and Cole, M. Literacy without schooling: Testing for intellectual effects. *Harvard Educational Review,* 1978, *48,* 448-461.

Sinclair, J. McH., and Coulthard, R.M. *Towards an analysis of discourse.* London: Oxford University Press, 1975.

Singer, H., and Donlan, D. *Reading and learning from text.* Hillsdale, NJ: Erlbaum, 1985.

Smith, F. Making sense of reading – and of reading instruction. *Harvard Educational Review,* 1977, *47,* 386-395.

Smith, F. *Understanding reading,* second edition. New York: Holt, Rinehart & Winston, 1978.

Smith, N.B. *American reading instruction.* Newark, DE: International Reading Association, 1965, 1986.

Snow, C., and Ferguson, C. (Eds.). *Talking to children: Language input and acquisition.* Cambridge, England: Cambridge University Press, 1977.

Sticht, T.G. *Reading for working.* Alexandria, VA: Human Resources Research Organization, 1975.

Stubbs, M. *Language, schools, and classroom.* London: Methuen, 1976.

Sulzby, E. Kindergartners as writers and readers. In M. Farr (Ed.), *Advances in writing research, volume 1: Children's early writing development.* Norwood, NJ: Ablex, 1985.

Tannen, D. What's in a frame? Surface evidence for underlying expectations. In R. Freedle (Ed.), *Advances in discourse processing,* volume 2. Norwood, NJ: Ablex, 1979.

Taylor, D. *Family literacy: Young children learning to read and write.* Portsmouth, NH: Heinemann, 1983.

Teale, W.H., and Sulzby, E. (Eds.). *Emergent literacy: Writing and reading.* Norwood, NJ: Ablex, 1986.

Tucker, G.R. The development of reading skills within a bilingual program. In S.S. Smiley and J.C. Towner (Eds.), *Sixth western symposium on learning: Language and reading.* Bellingham, WA: Western Washington State College, 1975, 49-60.

Vygotsky, L.S. *Mind in society.* Cambridge, MA: Harvard University Press, 1978.

Vygotsky, L.S. *Thought and language.* Cambridge, MA: MIT Press, 1977.

Watson, B. *An observation study of teaching beginning reading to new entrant children.* Unpublished master's thesis, University of Auckland, 1980.

Watson, D., and Bixby, M. Teachers! A support group needs you. *Georgia Journal of Reading*, Spring 1985, 13-17.

Wayson, W.W., Mitchell, B., Pinnell, G.S., and Landis, D. *Up from excellence: The impact of the excellence movement on schools*. Bloomington, IN: Phi Delta Kappa, 1988.

Weber, R. First graders' use of grammatical context in reading. In H. Levin and J.P. Williams (Eds.), *Basic studies on reading*. New York: Basic Books, 1970, 147-163.

Wells, G. *The meaning makers: Children learning language and using language to learn*. Portsmouth, NH: Heinemann, 1986.

Wells, G., in collaboration with A. Bridges, P. French, M. MacLure, C. Sinka, V. Walkerdine, and B. Wall. *Learning through interaction: The study of language development*. Cambridge, England: Cambridge University Press, 1981.

Witherell, C.S., and Erickson, L.V. Teacher education as adult development. *Theory into Practice*, 1978, *17*, 229-238.